IRELAND AND THE COMMONWEALTH:

TOWARDS MEMBERSHIP

Ireland and the Commonwealth:

Towards Membership

First published in 2009 by The Reform Group, and available worldwide.

Copyright © 2009 The Reform Group

ISBN: 978-0-9561577-1-3

Front Cover: Photograph by Kenroy Ambris, Commonwealth Secretariat.

This book is sold subject to the condition that it shall not, by way of trade or otherwise, be lent, re-sold, hired out or otherwise circulated without the publisher's prior consent in any form of binding or cover other than that in which it is published and without a similar condition including this condition being imposed on the subsequent purchaser.

All rights reserved. No part of this publication may be reproduced, stored in a retrieval system, or transmitted, in any form or by any means, electronic, mechanical, photocopying, or otherwise, without the prior permission of the publishers.

"The Commonwealth is a triumph of true human interests over the divisions of race, colour, culture and religion ... it represents a principle that transcends narrow interests and divisions and ... works to translate the concept of common humanity into a living reality."

-Chief Anyaoku, former Secretary-General of the Commonwealth

IRELAND AND THE COMMONWEALTH

ACKNOWLEDGEMENTS

Without the help and support of many, this collection would not have seen the light of day. The strategic mind of Professor Geoff Roberts led to the publishing of the Statement of support and to the successful Conference on the subject. The creative work of Mark C. Ryan in developing the 'Ireland and the Commonwealth' website[1], sparked the idea to have an accompanying book. The enthusiasm and willingness, which met requests to collect the following articles, speeches, and reports into one publication, is testimony to the enduring desire of those involved, to see Ireland back within the Commonwealth. We are indebted to Bruce

---

[1] http://www.irelandandthecommonwealth.com/

Arnold, Paedar Cassidy, John Erskine, Roy Garland, Mary Kenny, Andrew MacKinlay MP, Gordon Lucy, Prof. Robert Martin, John-Paul McCarthy, Sir Shridath Ramphal and Jerry Walsh for their interest and contribution to this important work. Special thanks are due to the Commonwealth Secretariat for their continued cooperation and assistance, and in particular, to Mr Amitav Banerji, Director of Political Affairs Division. We are also grateful to Dr Martin Mansergh, TD, Minister of State at the Department of Finance and the Arts, for his contribution to the debate.

Our hope is that this publication will help to inform, engage and inspire the political class and the public at large, of the cultural, political, and competitive sporting opportunities of Ireland returning to the Commonwealth.

Robin Bury
Chairman of The Reform Group

S.T.R. Gamble
Special Advisor
8th December 2009

FOREWORD	11
INTRODUCTION	15
TIME IS RIGHT FOR DEBATE	21
DOES THE COMMONWEALTH WORK FOR IRELAND?	28
REJOINING THE COMMONWEALTH WOULD BE GOOD FOR IRELAND	41
TOWARDS AN IRISH RETURN	50
WHY IRELAND HAS NOTHING TO LOSE IN REJOINING	59
WHY DID IRELAND LEAVE THE COMMONWEALTH?	66
CEIST AN CHOMHLATHAIS	74
FOR BETTER OR WORSE	77
WHAT IF?	88
WESTMINSTER HALL COMMONWEALTH DEBATE	112
AN END TO 60 YEARS OF SEPARATION?	124
THE COMMONWEALTH AT 60	130
THE QUEEN'S COMMONWEALTH DAY MESSAGE 2009	137
CELEBRATING THE COMMONWEALTH AT 60	140
IRELAND: TIME TO COME HOME	144
TIME TO RETURN	155

IRELAND AND THE COMMONWEALTH

FOREWORD

By Roy Garland
PEACE ACTIVIST AND IRISH NEWS COLUMNIST

This book is composed of a series of articles, speeches, letters and discussions generally supportive of Ireland's return to membership of the Commonwealth after a 60 year absence. During the intervening years Ireland has changed rapidly and so has the Commonwealth. The time now seems ripe for a return. A precedent exists in that South Africa joined in 1931, left in 1961 and returned to full membership in 1994.

A conference was organised by the Reform Group in Dublin and backed up by initiatives from Professor Geoff Roberts and other academics, columnists and writers. A supportive letter signed by people North and South was published in the Irish Times on Monday 23 March 2009. This was followed by a public discussion at the Camden Court Hotel, Dublin on Saturday 28th March 2009. The meeting was chaired by Irish News columnist and peace activist Roy Garland. Speakers included, Mr Amitav Banerji, Director Political Affairs Division, Commonwealth Secretariat, London, Dr Martin Mansergh Irish Minister of State, and Mr John Waters author and columnist with the Irish Times. Ms Antoinette Rademan, Political Counsellor, South African Embassy and Ms Ruth Farrugia, Chargé d'Affaires, Embassy of Malta, both spoke strongly in favour from the floor.

A surprising amount of reaction was positive but others seemed apathetic. The apathy could be interpreted as defeatism and it exists in both traditions. Too many Irish nationalists fail to appreciate that radical changes have taken place in the Commonwealth and few can see the potential in Ireland's return. Some hard line nationalists interpret any return as a return to British domination. For them the Commonwealth remains the British Commonwealth which of course it is not. On the unionist side, many would suspect that any return was motivated by a clever strategy of an imperialistic Ireland to re-gain the fourth green field.

Neither perspective is correct but ancient prejudices and emotions cloud judgements. An attempt is therefore made to face the issues dispassionately in the following pages. From my own perspective, which is that of a progressive Northern Unionist, new hope would lie in Ireland's return to the Commonwealth. Genuine healing of the dysfunctional relationships that have plagued this island for far too long would then become possible. But to achieve this would require courageous leadership from both traditions. Only a dynamic new leadership with vision could release us from the sterility of past dissensions and present discord.

It should never be forgotten that Irish people played a significant role in building the old Commonwealth. And because of this background Ireland could play a vital role in re-shaping the modern Commonwealth and fostering a better world for all future generations. Historically members of both Irish traditions have engaged in overseas aid work. Because of this island's unique history, we are well placed to build new relationships. The Commonwealth would enable Irish people to play an even bigger role in peace-making missions worldwide. In this way we could maintain the solid legacy of constructive relationships with other nations. Together we could begin to face up to the global problems that now threaten our planet.

Roy Garland,

7th December 2009

INTRODUCTION

On 23rd March 2009, this statement was signed in the Irish Republic and Northern Ireland supporting Ireland's entry into the Commonwealth and published in the Irish Times.

As Ireland approaches the 60th anniversary of the declaration of the Republic, is it time to reconsider the country's membership of the Commonwealth? When Ireland left the Commonwealth in 1949 the other member states hoped that its departure would be temporary. In the 1920s and 1930s the Irish Free State had played a crucial role in the transformation of the British Commonwealth into an association of free, democratic and sovereign states. After Ireland left, the Commonwealth continued to evolve. The 1949 London declaration ended the bar on Republics being members of the Commonwealth and dropped "British" from its title. By agreement of the member states the Queen remained Head of the Commonwealth, but only as the symbol of a free association of independent countries. In the 1950s and 1960s Commonwealth membership served as a bridge to world affairs for many newly sovereign states in Asia, Africa, and the Caribbean. Today the Commonwealth is an international organisation of 53[2] states committed to peace, democracy, human rights, racial equality, sustainable development, and the rule of law. No less than 32 of these states are Republics.

Commonwealth membership would be good for Ireland and good for the Commonwealth. Ireland and the Commonwealth stand for the same values in international relations. Members of the Commonwealth share a common heritage and history, including an Irish diaspora of some 20 million people – an international community that seems certain to grow as many people are forced by economic circumstances to emigrate from Ireland. Ireland's membership of the Commonwealth would strengthen its links with a vast network of countries, communities, civic

---

[2] On 28 November 2009, Commonwealth leaders holding their biennial Commonwealth Heads of Government Meeting (CHOGM) in Port of Spain, Trinidad and Tobago, agreed to admit the Republic of Rwanda as the 54th member of the Commonwealth, and 33rd republic.

associations and professional bodies. Ireland – with its extensive and respected experience of UN and EU peacekeeping activities - could make an important contribution to the Commonwealth's efforts to promote democracy, prevent conflict, and protect human rights. The Commonwealth represents an important body of international public opinion and an opportunity for Ireland to strengthen its voice and influence in the global arena.

Among the many practical advantages of membership of the Commonwealth is the right to compete in the Commonwealth Games – the only multinational, multisport event apart from the Olympics. The next games will be held in India in 2010. Ireland's participation in those games would be good preparation for the London Olympics in 2012.

Membership of the Commonwealth is more relevant than ever as Ireland faces its worst economic crisis since the foundation of the state. The county is going to need all the friends and connections it can get in the perilous economic times that lie ahead. The Commonwealth is not an alternative or substitute for Ireland's membership of other international bodies such as the EU or the UN but it could prove to be an invaluable addition if our worst fears about the global economic crisis are fulfilled.

Ireland's membership of the Commonwealth would, we are sure, be welcomed by the unionist community in Northern Ireland as significant gesture of reconciliation. It would add to the collaborative framework established by the Belfast and St Andrew's agreements. It would demonstrate unequivocally that the Republic has finally drawn a line under the troubled history of Anglo-Irish relations that led to Ireland's self-exclusion from the Commonwealth 60 years ago. It would represent a further important step along the road to a pluralist Ireland in which different identities are recognised and respected, a country that celebrates its multi-cultural heritage and diverse history.

Roy Garland
Professor Geoffrey Roberts
Bruce Arnold
Ian Beamish
David Burnside MLA
Robin Bury
Anne Carr
David Christoper

Liam Clarke

Dr Brian Crowe

Professor Brice Dickson

Ruth Dudley Edwards

Gerald Fitzgerald

George Fleming

David Ford MLA

S.T.R. Gamble

Senator Eoghan Harris

Professor Liam Kennedy

Con Logue

Pierce Martin

Steven McColl

R.B. McDowell

Pamela McMillen

Aidan O'Hara

Roderick W Oliver

Simon Partridge

Dawn Purvis MLA

Lord Rana

Mark C. Ryan

William J. Sibbett

Derek Simpson

Dr Bill Smith

James Smyth

Tony Stanney

Jack Storey

Billy Tate MBE

David S.C. Thompson

Jerry Walsh

(All signatories in a personal capacity)

Time is Right for Debate

By Bruce Arnold

Author and Journalist

A good few years ago now, Sean Cantwell, the chief leader writer in the Irish Independent with whom I shared an office -- I was then the paper's literary editor -- asked me, would I mind if he said something personal? I said, not at all, thinking personal remarks were as good as any other kind and often better. He then regretted, on my behalf, my accent. "It might have been better if you spoke like Jack Charlton." I added: "It might also have helped if I had been a footballer!"

I have often thought of that encounter, not regretting it -- I am quite proud of my accent -- but I understood Sean Cantwell's view, that in the deeper backwoods of Irish political and religious culture, it was at times a trifle burdensome.

For the last half century, I have written always from within myself, my words reflecting views and beliefs. The views have always been Irish, concerned with the welfare of this country, whether political, artistic, moral or social. On the whole, they have been outspoken and challenging, which has to do with my nature.

The beliefs are rather different and reflect a position that has been unwavering. I am British, Protestant, and come from a dwindling and anachronistic class located somewhere between Kent, London and the Cotswolds. I have related something of the class I come from in my books, most notably in 'He That is Down Need Fear No Fall', published last year.

Despite these introductory words, this article tries to come to terms with a couple of recent events: firstly, the recent terrorist killings in Northern Ireland which struck a new chord in North-South relations, in Anglo-Irish relations, perhaps also in the relationships between two communities in the North and between the ragged remnants of those two points of view in the south.

Well before the killings, moves were afoot in the south to bring up an issue that has already attracted considerable interest and to hold a public debate -- on whether is it time to reconsider the country's membership of the Commonwealth.

Ireland is approaching the 60th anniversary of the declaration of the Republic. This was in the mind of the main organiser of the debate, Robin Bury, of the Reform Movement. I was patron of this organisation for a number of years and have had a long association with its founding figure. We share a deep concern for the Protestants in the south, on which Robin Bury is writing a book, his thesis based on the idea that the Protestant community in the Republic went under, was pacified, in the sense of separate identity, and then deracinated. I do not agree with this.

Small it may be, as a practising community, but it has never gone under.[3]

Another of the interests Robin Bury has is a liking for the Commonwealth and a belief in Ireland's return to membership. Martin Mansergh, Minister of State at the Department of Financewith special responsibility for the Office of Public Works, will debate this question a week from today.

Another speaker is Amitav Banerji, director of the political affairs division of the Commonwealth Secretariat in London, who was urged to attend by Commonwealth Secretary-General Kamalesh Sharma. John Waters of the 'Irish Times', will also speak and Roy Garland, a peace activist and a 'Irish News' columnist, will chair the event.

Martin Mansergh's presence is important on two grounds. Though only recently elected to the Dail, he has been consistently involved in Fianna Fail politics, firstly as a political adviser to Charles Haughey, particularly on Northern Ireland, and later as adviser to Albert Reynolds

---

[3] Robin Bury subsequently wrote a letter to the *Irish Independent* 23rd March pointing out that he had not maintained that the Protestant community in the South had gone under.

and Bertie Ahern. With his earlier experience in the Department of Foreign Affairs, he is uniquely placed to speak on the subject.

He will be giving an analysis, no doubt drawing certain sympathies and understandings derived from his father, Nicholas Mansergh, a distinguished historian with a lifelong interest in the British Commonwealth -- his first book, published in 1934, 'The Irish Free State: Its Government and Politics'. Mansergh Sr wrote of the Commonwealth:

"For my generation, the Commonwealth had much in common with the Common Market nowadays. I was interested in the Commonwealth to see if it would provide a way forward in Ireland itself. An inherent weakness in the Anglo-Irish Treaty was that the Dominion settlement was not consistent with Partition. I felt that Dominion status wouldn't work, which was obvious enough by 1934, but I wasn't sure whether any alternative to Dominion status would work in Ireland's case."

Martin Mansergh still sees this as an emotive issue and possibly divisive. For many, it would be coloured by views on a united Ireland, though he wouldn't be an advocate, but he will be contributing to a better understanding of the issues.

To have Amitav Banerji present as well is an added bonus since it will add emphasis to the good analogies between Europe and Commonwealth countries. In addition, there are the Commonwealth commitment to democracy and good governance, human rights and the rule of law, gender equality and sustainable economic and social development.

When Ireland left the Commonwealth in 1949, the other member states hoped that its departure would be temporary since, in the 1920s and 1930s, the Irish Free State had played a crucial role in the transformation of the British Commonwealth into an association of free, democratic and sovereign states. Since then, it stopped being the 'British' Commonwealth and the monarch as its head is only symbolic.

Robin Bury, of the Reform Movement, has said: "Membership of the Commonwealth is more relevant than ever." He cites the economic crisis as one of the reasons. "The country is going to need all the friends and connections it can get in the perilous economic times that lie ahead.

"Ireland's membership of the Commonwealth would be welcomed by the unionist community in Northern Ireland as significant gesture of reconciliation . . . It would demonstrate unequivocally that the Republic has finally drawn a line under the troubled history of Anglo-Irish relations [and] would represent a further important step along the road to a pluralist Ireland."

Perhaps, indeed, we should rethink our position.[4]

---

[4] This article was published in *Irish Independent*, 21 March 2009.

Does the Commonwealth work for Ireland?

By Amitav Banerji

DIRECTOR OF POLITICAL AFFAIRS DIVISION, COMMONWEALTH SECRETARAIT

Speech delivered at the 'Ireland and Commonwealth Conference' at Camden Court Hotel, Dublin, 28th March 2009.

It is seven years ago almost to the day that I was here last. On that occasion too, I was earning my keep spreading the gospel of the Commonwealth. But I was then preaching to the converted – to Commonwealth Ambassadors, as it happens. This congregation, and this occasion, are different.

Today's conference has a more special significance, because of its theme, and because of the confluence of two anniversaries. In just over two weeks, it will be sixty years since Ireland formally departed from the Commonwealth. And in about four weeks it will be sixty years since the Commonwealth as we know it, was born.

That paradox is, of course, easily resolved. Ireland left the British Commonwealth on 14 April 1949. The British Commonwealth officially faded into history on 26 April 1949, and the modern Commonwealth was born, delivered by the London Declaration of Commonwealth Prime Ministers of that date.

So the Commonwealth that Ireland left no longer officially exists. Your debate here today is about whether or not it should consider joining a different Commonwealth. It is one of the enormous ironies of history that Ireland played a major part in shaping the Commonwealth that it chose to leave, and that it did so literally days before India was allowed to remain as a republic, thus opening the Commonwealth's doors to so many other republics in time to come.

I am privileged to be part of this debate, but I must be careful. While I earn my living as a flag-bearer for the Commonwealth, and you would therefore expect me to say good things about it, it would not be right for me to get drawn into either supporting or opposing the motion before you.

Whether Ireland seeks to rejoin the Commonwealth or not is a question for Irish policy makers and the Irish people, not for pontification by outsiders. It is a complex question, wrapped in considerations of history, geography, economics, faith, culture and very deep and raw emotion. North, south, east and west, all have their own special meaning in the Irish context. No outsider can get beyond a superficial understanding of these complexities at best.

What I can do is to enable you to have an informed debate and make a conscious choice. That is my mission this morning.

Until the republic was proclaimed on Easter Day 1949 - some say even earlier, when the External Relations Act was repealed -- the Commonwealth was a collection of nine.

Without Ireland, it was reduced to eight. Those were all Dominions, with King George VI as their Head of State.

Today, it is a grouping of 53 countries, 32 of which are republics and only 16 of which still treat Queen Elizabeth II as their Head of State. The remaining five have their own monarchs. Ireland thus left a small group that grew in membership to a number six times as large, and one that others are still seeking to join.

The Commonwealth today is not a uni-polar, anglo-centric organisation, even if the UK remains a key member and the largest financial contributor. It offers each member a window to 52 others. It is thus a truly global organisation, with an enormous diversity of members.

They range from affluent G-8 members like UK and Canada, to major emerging economies like India, Malaysia and South Africa, to micro-states in the Pacific and Caribbean. We have large and small, rich and poor, island and landlocked. We can claim virtually every ethnic, religious and linguistic group. And we work on the basis of consensus.

It is also important to point out that, in 1965, the Secretariat of the Commonwealth ceased to be located in the British Government and became an impartial, multi-nations organisation, answerable to the membership in its totality. Today it has about 280 employees from some 37 countries.

The value of consensus in such a diverse organisation is self-evident. On a number of issues in the past, the Commonwealth had demonstrated that it can help mould consensus on current issues. Its Langkawi Declaration on the Environment of 1989 strongly influenced the Rio Earth Summit Declaration of 1992. It was Commonwealth Finance Ministers that came up with the idea of the Heavily Indebted Poor Countries (HIPC) initiative. More recently, our Marlborough House Statement on reform of international institutions of June 2008 influenced both the outcome of the Washington G-20 summit and the UN's Doha Conference on Financing for Development.

Where the Commonwealth has truly established a global brand image is in the field of democracy and good governance. In 1991, it adopted the Harare Commonwealth Declaration, which defined the fundamental political values of the Commonwealth to include democracy, democratic processes and institutions which reflect national circumstances, the rule of law and the independence of the judiciary, just and honest government, fundamental human rights and equality for women.

Four years later, the Commonwealth gave teeth to that Declaration, by setting out agreed measures for dealing with serious or persistent violations of the Harare Principles and created a ministerial body to serve as their custodian. The Commonwealth Ministerial Action Group (CMAG) has often used its teeth to bite hard.

Several countries have been suspended from the councils of the Commonwealth from time to time. Some have been reinstated, but only after a democratically elected government was restored. Zimbabwe did not accept its suspension and walked out of the Commonwealth. Fiji is currently under suspension.

So the Commonwealth no longer pays mere lip service to democracy. Since 1991, twelve countries have moved from military or one party-rule to multi-party democracy. We help our members in many ways, from observing elections, to building or buttressing democratic institutions. Our sister organisation, the Commonwealth Parliamentary Association, is one of our most important partners in this endeavour.

No other global organisation can match this record in terms of the progress of democracy.

Others have followed where the Commonwealth has led. The Harare Declaration has been replicated now by several other international organisations. Just last week the African Union suspended Madagascar, a step unimaginable even a few years ago.

The point I am seeking to establish is that there is no place in the Commonwealth any more for dictators and autocrats. In our organisation, leaders elected through the ballot box don't like sharing a forum with those who have found their way to power through the barrel of a gun. You cannot get away any more with large scale violations of human rights, or the rule of law, or of the freedom of expression. And you cannot be admitted into membership of the Commonwealth if you cannot demonstrate that you abide by these basic principles.

This is a good point for me to mention the criteria and processes that govern applications for Commonwealth membership. These were agreed at the last Commonwealth summit in Kampala, Uganda, in 2007. For any country to be admitted o membership, it must meet the following core criteria:

1. It should, as a general rule, have had a historic constitutional association with an existing Commonwealth member, save in exceptional circumstances;

2. In exceptional circumstances, applications should be considered on a case-by-case basis;

3. An applicant country should accept and comply with Commonwealth fundamental values, principles and

priorities as set out in the 1971 Declaration of Commonwealth principles and in other subsequent Declarations;

4. It must demonstrate commitment to: democracy and democratic processes, including free and fair elections and representative legislatures; the rule of law and independence of the judiciary; good governance, including a well-trained public service and transparent public accounts; and protection of human rights, freedom of expression, and equality of opportunity;

5. The country should accept Commonwealth norms and conventions, such as the use of the English language as the medium of inter-Commonwealth relations, and acknowledge Queen Elizabeth II as the Head of the Commonwealth; and

6. New members should be encouraged to join the Commonwealth Foundation, and to promote vigorous civil society and business organisations within their countries, and to foster participatory democracy through regular civil society consultations.

A four-step process was also approved for considering applications for membership: the applicant country must first submit itself to an informal assessment of the ability of a country to meet the criteria. This is followed by consultation with existing members. A formal application is then encouraged if warranted, for consideration by Heads of Government. A joint resolution from the applicant country's legislature can help the case.

While democracy is one pillar of the Commonwealth, development is the other. The two go hand in hand and are mutually reinforcing. Socio-economic growth and wealth creation are promoted through education, the empowerment of women and young people, building trade capacity, promoting private investment, assisting debt management, and in many other ways. It is not always realized that nearly 25% of global trade takes place within the Commonwealth. And that over 20% of investment flows are also intra-Commonwealth.

The Commonwealth may not have the economic clout of the European Union, but it has some of the fastest growing economies of the world. According to the Commonwealth

Business Council, doing business in another Commonwealth country, using the English language, taking advantage of similar corporate legal frameworks and accounting practices, can deliver up to a 15% cost advantage.

A measure of the enormous trust and confidence the Commonwealth enjoys is to be found in the extent to which member countries invite the Commonwealth to help them resolve domestic political issues that could cause conflict and endanger national stability. We call it the Good Offices role of the Secretary-General. They have been employed in Guyana, Cameroon, Swaziland, Maldives, Fiji and Tonga, to name a few. This often happens quietly and behind the scenes. Good offices and megaphone diplomacy do not readily mix.

Many do not realise how large the Commonwealth family actually is. The inter-governmental organisation for which I work is only a small, albeit important, part of that family. There are close to 90 organisations that bear the Commonwealth name - Commonwealth parliamentarians, journalists, magistrates and judges, lawyers, doctors, nurses... They are all a vital part of this rich tapestry.

I cannot fail to mention the Commonwealth Games, known familiarly as the 'Friendly Games'. This is the great four-yearly effervescence of the Commonwealth spirit on the sporting fields. The next Games take place in New Delhi in 2010, with Glasgow to follow in 2014.

I should also mention that the Commonwealth is the only global organisation that has a dedicated Youth Programme. Indeed the theme for our 60th anniversary this year is *The Commonwealth@60 - Serving a New Generation.*

There is another quality that positions the Commonwealth well as an organisation of the future. It is the ability to manage diversity. I firmly believe that the problems of tomorrow are going to stem from divides of various kinds - economic, ethnic, religious, cultural. On the one hand, the world continues to shrink. On the other, societies continue to become more fractured. The Commonwealth recognizes that diversity needs to be harnessed in a positive way and in 2007 a commission headed by Professor Amartya Sen produced a monumental report, Civil Paths to Peace, to suggest ways of doing so.

In 1948, with the world moving into the throes of a Cold War, Prime Minister Nehru spoke of the Commonwealth as providing 'a touch of healing'. Forty six years later, Nelson Mandela famously remarked, 'The Commonwealth makes the world safe for diversity'.

So the Commonwealth is a vibrant, contemporary, relevant and credible organisation that Irish policy makers of the late 1940s may not readily recognise today. It is flexible and not hide-bound. It does not have a charter, but relies heavily on traditions and conventions. It has a strong sense of 'family', helped of course by a shared language that is now the preferred medium of global discourse. And it is a partnership of equals, which respects the sovereignty of each member.

Does the Commonwealth work for Ireland? That is a question only Ireland can answer!

Rejoining the Commonwealth would be good for Ireland

By Professor Robert Martin

Professor of Law, Emeritus, University of Western Ontario
and an Honorary Fellow of Trinity College Dublin

The Republic should consider rejoining the Commonwealth - both for itself and the confidence-building it would help promote with unionists, argues Robert Martin. The Commonwealth today is not, as many Irish people imagine it to be, the British Empire in drag; it is not the resurrected cadaver of empire. It is over half a century since Ireland left the Commonwealth. It's time for the Irish to take another look.

In 1997, in one of her last public acts as president of Ireland, Mary Robinson suggested that Ireland should seriously consider rejoining the Commonwealth. In 1998, writing in The Irish Times, Fintan O'Toole made a similar suggestion. The Taoiseach recently expressed a similar view.

The first step in thinking about the modern Commonwealth, the Commonwealth of today, is gaining a clear understanding of what it is not.

The simplest way of affirming this is to reflect on what the position would be today if the perception of the Commonwealth as the warmed-over corpse of empire were accurate. If it were, no one would give a damn about the Commonwealth. But many, many people in every corner of the earth do care about the Commonwealth. The reality must be different.

Arnold Smith, the Canadian who became the Commonwealth's first secretary general in 1965, described it as an organisation formed by the leaders of national liberation movements.

Who were those leaders? Jawaharlal Nehru (India), Julius Nyerere (Tanzania), Kenneth Kaunda (Zambia), Eric

Williams (Trinidad), Robert Mugabe (Zimbabwe) and Nelson Mandela (South Africa). Hardly the people one would imagine to be supporters of British imperialism in disguise.

And does belonging to the organisation they created mean accepting a sort of recolonisation? The Commonwealth has not been "British" since 1949, when that adjective, with all it implied, was formally dropped from the organisation's name. Many Irish people and, unfortunately, many Canadians have yet to grasp this simple point.

Would Commonwealth membership mean that the British queen would acquire some authority over Ireland? Not even remotely. Commonwealth membership does not require accepting the British monarch as head of state. There are 54 countries in the Commonwealth. Of these, no fewer than 33 are republics. Five have their own monarchs. Only 16 out of 54 retain Queen Elizabeth as their head of state.

The key figure in the Commonwealth's administrative structure is the secretary general. Five persons have occupied this post - one from Canada, one from Guyana, one from Nigeria, one from New Zealand and the incumbent from India. Still, for what it's worth, the Commonwealth secretariat is located in London.

And Queen Elizabeth has the title "Head of the Commonwealth". The idea that this title gives her any authority - authority to interfere in the affairs of say, Uganda, would, I suspect, be both surprising and amusing to the President of Uganda. Neither the name nor likeness of the English queen appears on any of the national symbols of those Commonwealth states which are republics.

After understanding what the Commonwealth is not, it is necessary to ask, what is it?. There are, in fact, two Commonwealths: the official Commonwealth and the unofficial - or people's - Commonwealth.

The story of the modern Commonwealth began in 1926 with the Balfour Declaration. That document described the Commonwealth as a free association of equal states, "in no way subordinate one to another". The Statute of Westminster of 1931 formally removed any remaining legal fetters on the independence of Commonwealth states.

The two countries most responsible for forcing these changes in the Commonwealth were Canada and Ireland.

The London Declaration of 1949 removed the word "British" from the organisation's name and set out the constitutional formula which made it possible for republics to retain Commonwealth membership.

But the London Declaration came only eight days after Ireland announced that, upon becoming a republic, it would leave the Commonwealth.

In 1965 a formal structure for the Commonwealth was adopted. That structure is simple. Policy is set by the heads of government who meet every two years. The Commonwealth Secretariat's job is to carry out those policy decisions.

The secretariat includes divisions devoted to Legal and Constitutional Affairs, Information and Public Affairs, Science and Technology, Human Resource Development and Gender and Youth Affairs. The secretariat also administers a fund which is used for investment in development co-operation.

In 1971 heads of government meeting in Singapore adopted a Declaration of Commonwealth Principles. Central to these principles were a commitment to equality and a rejection of racism and colonialism. Hostility towards racism and racial division is the touchstone of the Commonwealth.

And the Commonwealth's finest hour came in the next decades. It was unstinting in its opposition to settler rule in Zimbabwe and to apartheid in South Africa and in its support for the people seeking to achieve democracy in those countries.

The People's Commonwealth is a network of agencies, non-governmental organisations, and ordinary men and women.

The range of organisations involved is extraordinary, from the Association of Commonwealth Archivists and Record Managers to the Commonwealth Dental Association and the Commonwealth Trade Union Council.

While the unofficial Commonwealth does a lot of good work, what is does may not be as important as how it does it. The Commonwealth's style is unique.

We live in a dangerously fractured world. The Commonwealth actively addresses those fractures. At Commonwealth gatherings men and women from all parts of the world meet as equals and in mutual respect to address issues of common concern.

In February of 1998 I was at a meeting at the Commonwealth secretariat. We sat around a magnificent 18th century wooden table. We came from Australia, Canada, Gambia, Jamaica, India, Malawi, Nigeria, South Africa and the UK. With a handful of exceptions, none of us had ever met before.

Our task was to devise a programme for implementation throughout the Commonwealth, to enhance access to justice. The meeting was to last two days. We talked. We exchanged experiences and points of view. And we came up with a programme which was both solid and practical. This is the way the People's Commonwealth usually works.

Commonwealth membership would be good for Ireland and good for the Commonwealth. It would mean building on what already exists. As is the case, for example, with

Irish aid. All but one of the priority recipient countries for Irish aid are Commonwealth members.

Membership would lead to extending the range of direct government-to-government and people-to- people contacts. It would mean copper-fastening current ties and being able to create a host of new ones.

I have argued that the perception of the Commonwealth as British is inaccurate and out of date and that the reality is quite different. But like it or not, perceptions, no matter how inaccurate, can be significant.

The inaccurate perception that the Commonwealth remains British could be used to Ireland's benefit. There has been much talk of the need for confidence-building measures to encourage the peace process in the six counties of the North.

A statement that the Irish Government was committed to rejoining the Commonwealth could be a significant confidence-building measure.

The Commonwealth is an international organisation. It is not an alliance. Membership in the Commonwealth would in no way compromise Ireland's much-cherished neutrality.

The Commonwealth consists of developed and developing countries, of First World nations and of Third World nations.

Ireland would be the only developed, Western member of the Commonwealth to have experienced both colonialism and a struggle for independence. When Zimbabweans speak of colonialism, the oppression of minority rule and the struggle to revive national culture, their experiences resonate with Irish history.

There is a natural bond between Ireland and the Asian, African and Caribbean countries of the Commonwealth. It should be strengthened and institutionalised. Commonwealth membership would be the best means of achieving these ends.[5]

---

[5] This article was published in *Irish Times*, 23rd November 2001.

TOWARDS AN IRISH RETURN

BY MARY KENNY
AUTHOR AND JOURNALIST

"It would enlarge Ireland's influence to join the Commonwealth – and enhance the sense of inclusivity in the Irish nation..."

I love Irish history and I regard myself as a patriotic Irishwoman: but I passionately believe that one of the most important projects for the future of our country is that the Irish nation, in its historical perspective as well as in its cultural reach, should constantly work towards becoming, and being, truly inclusive. Sometimes, in the early forging of a new state, that state focuses too narrowly on what is perceived as its national heritage: there is a regrettably history of new states – Central Europe after the

Great War being a prime example – liberating themselves from great empires, and promptly turning against their own minorities. Nationalism can be narrow-minded, and can too easily exclude those who do not seem to fit into the national narrative, which may touch on some crackpot theory of racial or ethnic "purity".

Sometimes there is an element of retrospective historical compensation, or over-compensation, as when triumphant nationalists seek to take revenge on those who they considered, previously, their lords and masters. A crude example of this was when Dan Breen, the IRA gunman, swore: "We'll get every f****** Orangeman out of the country!", which also meant, to the misguided mentality of some of his followers, behaving atrociously towards harmless Protestants in West Cork. (In any case, earlier Irish republicans had included "Orangemen" within the Irish narrative.)

There are examples of historical payback: in the early years of the 20th century, the Irish Catholic newspaper (then owned by William Martin Murphy, the entrepreneur) consistently complained that Catholics in Dublin were disbarred from advancement in employment under the Crown. There was a grain of truth in this – some Chief Secretaries, such as Walter Long, certainly insisted on only hiring "sound Unionists" for government jobs: but let us call this a previous failure to be inclusive.

In contrast, speaking in the famous Treaty debate of 1922, Arthur Griffith gave a wise and generous lead to the country when he spoke about meeting with the Anglo-Irish, and those who were Southern Unionists by conviction or tradition. "I met them," he said, "because they are my countrymen; and because, if we are to have an Irish nation, we want to start with fair play for all sections and with understanding between all sections." He was widely applauded for this, and more applause followed when he said he would meet the Ulster Unionists for the same reason – to promise them "fair play", and as far as he was concerned they would have such fair play from the Irish nation. (Ironically, the person who heckled this speech vociferously was Countess Markievicz, the former Constance Gore-Booth, who came from a Southern Unionist family herself – though always, it seemed, in rebellion against her own folks.)

In the years following, as the Irish Free State developed, it was, of course, initially part of the British Commonwealth of nations, and indeed Eire, as the Twenty-Six Counties was subsequently called, played an active role within that family of nations. When the Irish Free State insisted on choosing its own Governor-General – the first being Tim Healy, of the Irish Parliamentary Party – rather than passively accepting London's nominee, the Canadians and Australia's felt that this was a modernising innovation.

The Statute of Westminster, enacted in 1931, widened the autonomy of the Dominions, and in effect rendered the Imperial Parliament in London merely "first among equals", rather than the dominant power: some historians have suggested that Eire's influence within the Commonwealth helped to usher in this progressive demarche.

In some respects the Irish Free State contained an unexpectedly modernising aspect, despite its strong traditionalism in areas associated with values and morals. For example, De Valera's Constitution of 1937, although certainly couched in some of the mystical language associated with Dev, nonetheless had these modernising elements – a concept of "human rights", for example, which the UN charter would not instigate until 1948: and a flexibility to delete and replace clauses and articles which became outdated, or objectionable.

Thus the "special position" accorded to the Catholic church in the 1937 version of the Constitution – arguably somewhat sectarian, although it did accord with the social perception at the time – was quite rightly deleted in 1972. (Some secular critics today would wish to delete the preamble to the Constitution, which begins "In the Name of the Most Holy Trinity, from Whom is all authority, and to Whom, as our final end, all actions both of men and States must be referred". Yet again, ironically, the Trinity was invoked because in 1937, that was considered an "inclusive" symbol – certainly inclusive to all Trinitarian Christians.It can, obviously, be deleted, if there is a democratic will to do so.)

After the Constitution was enacted, the King was, it seemed erased from relations between London and Dublin, except in the most tenuous sense – as head of the

Commonwealth. The final break, as we all know, came with the Inter-Party government headed by John Costello in 1948-49, although much of the impetus for declaring a Republic came from Sean MacBride, as Minister For External affairs, and (as the son of Maud Gonne and John MacBride, the pro-Boer veteran) an ardent republican. De Valera, in all his canniness, repudiated this break with Crown and Commonwealth and refused to attend the celebrations marking the Republic at Easter 1949. Despite his often contentious relations with London in the 1930s and 40s – sometimes downright mean-spirited, as when he forbade Irish diplomats in London to celebrate the Coronation in 1937 and forbade his own Party members to attend any royal occasion – nevertheless, Dev always insisted that he would have retained the link with the Commonwealth.

Firstly, the Commonwealth is a world forum, and small countries need a world forum. Secondly, and perhaps more importantly, for the Irish nation, the Commonwealth always had the potential for bridge-building with Northern Ireland.

That break should never have happened: certainly not if we want a truly inclusive society, which I think most people on the island of Ireland do. The challenge now is to rebuild that whole relationship, within the context of inclusiveness, and for the sake of the future. And that, I think, probably needs a programme of information within the public realm in Ireland, explaining – even educating – the public about the Commonwealth today.

There would still be a certain kneejerk, let us say "old Fenian", view of the Commonwealth as a kind of closeted British imperialism: but that is not at all the way the modern, globalised Commonwealth is seen by its members. Indeed, the "leading" member of the Commonwealth today is often seen as India – a republic, as it happens, and a vast Asian democracy. The Commonwealth is emphatically multi-racial and multi-ethnic, as can be witnessed from the phalanx of Commonwealth leaders who gather together each November at the Cenotaph in London to honour the dead of the world wars. The Commonwealth can play a helpful and healing role in restoring problem states, such as Zimbabwe, to a working democracy, or help to put together a society broken by violence and genocide, such as Rwanda, an enthusiastic Commonwealth member.

The links Ireland has with so many of the other Commonwealth members derive not just from, say, emigration (as to Australia, New Zealand and Canada) and the Irish diaspora throughout the world, but also, interestingly through the history of the Irish Catholic Church, whose missions so often worked in Commonwealth countries. An organisation like the Medical Missionaries of Mary, set up by the Dublin nun, Mary Martin, is one of the most powerful providers of health throughout Africa and much of the Third World, also associated with Commonwealth links. Holy Ghost fathers from Ireland virtually set up the education system in a country like Sierra Leone: Irish Jesuits educated Mugabe himself (and might still have some influence with him). The Loreto nuns of Ireland had a huge network all over India, educating many Hindu girls in their own faith too. (Mother Teresa of Calcutta was, of course, a Loreto nun, trained at Rathfarnham, Co Dublin, before she started her own order.)

The Commonwealth today comprises 54 nations, representing 30 per cent of the world's population, and Ireland would have many historical, cultural and familial links with these countries. President Kennedy famously said that we should think not just what our country can do for us, but what we can do for our country: by the same token, think not just what the Commonwealth could do for Ireland (and it could help to make our whole island more inclusive) but what Ireland could also do for the Commonwealth. Some Commonwealth countries are, alas, perilously close to becoming failed States – there is much current concern about the breakdown of civil society in Pakistan. Ireland went through her own, sometimes thorny path of state-building in the 20th century, and could provide much collegiate advice and guidance in this area.

We must broaden this issue out, help to engender more public, well-informed discussion around it, and invite more democratic support for the practical and positive proposal to bring our country back into the active and prestigious Commonwealth of Nations.

Why Ireland has Nothing To Lose in Rejoining

By John-Paul McCarthy

IRISH HISTORIAN, UNIVERSITY OF OXFORD

In his playful and under-regarded memoir, Smile and be a Villain, Niall Toibin recalled the months he spent working as a lowly clerk in the Department of External Affairs after the end of the Second World War.

One of his fellow drones, Sean Gaynor, who later became an ambassador, apparently could do a wonderful rendition of minister Sean MacBride's adenoidal Parisian drawl. Toibin recalled that one day he was standing on a step ladder in his office, filing papers away with his back to the door, when he heard the familiar French voice which asked him a question along the lines of, "Niall, I wonder if it would be possible to . . ."

Without turning around, Toibin assumed it was his old pal up to his usual ventriloquising tricks, and simply said, "Sean, will you just f*** off with the MacBride routine, I'm very busy today." He turned around, only to see the back of the minister himself, walking off with some American journalist. "There was never a word about it," Toibin wrote. "The minister did not come back later on. He didn't say 'why did you tell me to f*** off?' He never batted an eyelid."

All of which goes to show that MacBride was a very odd man in many respects, and as we all reflect on the recent call for Ireland to reconsider our membership of the Commonwealth, we must confront the dubious legacy of his erratic tenure at External Affairs between 1948-51. Ireland abruptly left the Commonwealth on his watch, and refused to join Nato as well, since he thought our refusal here would somehow leverage the UK into 'ending partition' as a quid pro quo.

MacBride's delusional statecraft here haunts us still, and it is high time to think again about some of the benefits that could accrue to us should we rejoin the Commonwealth paddock where Irish diplomats came to carve out such a distinguished reputation in the Twenties and Thirties.

As the cogent letter to the Irish Times argued last week, "Today the Commonwealth is an international organisation of 53 states committed to peace, democracy, human rights, racial equality, sustainable development, and the rule of law. No fewer than 32 of these states are republics.

"Commonwealth membership would be good for Ireland and good for the Commonwealth. Ireland and the Commonwealth stand for the same values in international relations. Members of the Commonwealth share a common heritage and history, including an Irish diaspora of some 20 million people -- an international community that seems certain to grow as many people are forced by economic circumstances to emigrate from Ireland."

"Ireland's membership of the Commonwealth would strengthen its links with a vast network of countries, communities, civic associations and professional bodies."

"Ireland -- with its extensive and respected experience of UN and EU peacekeeping activities -- could make an important contribution to the Commonwealth's efforts to promote democracy, prevent conflict and protect human rights."

This is another way of arguing that there need be no diminution in our status as a sovereign state, or any tugging of the forelock should we decide to rejoin. Rather, membership here would merely give some institutional form to the profound Anglophilia which has characterised Irish patriotic thinking between O'Connell and de Valera, both of whom greatly admired the liberal, democratic values which they saw as inherent in British constitutional tradition since the Glorious Revolution in the 17th century. In important ways, their careers were not rejections of the British inheritance rather than campaigns to have Ireland enjoy the fruits of this inheritance, as equal partners.

De Valera himself rather relished the spotlight of the Commonwealth stage, as well the influence that he was able to exert on such mighty democracies as India.

After all, as the historian Nicholas Mansergh reminds us, he personally advised the first prime minister of independent India, Jawaharlal Nehru, to keep India within the Commonwealth, while also proudly declaring itself a federal, secular republic.

He was reluctant to take Ireland fully out of the Commonwealth because of his sensitivity to unionists' concerns, a laudable and humane calculation however misplaced his emphasis might have been in practice, though.

The career of the maverick Canadian prime minister from the Seventies, Pierre Elliott Trudeau is worth recalling in the context of this Commonwealth debate. He shows that we have nothing to lose in rejoining, and potentially a lot to gain across a whole range of issues, be they economic, cultural or diplomatic.

Trudeau was a Catholic French speaker, and he began his premiership in 1968 expressing deep suspicion of the Commonwealth, with its imperial fripperies and geo-strategic mumbo-jumbo. And yet, this tough-minded, Canadian patriot came to greatly value his role on the Commonwealth stage within less than a decade in power.

He used his Commonwealth pulpit to harangue Margaret Thatcher very effectively on apartheid, and Ronald Reagan came to dread his high-octane lectures on the moral necessity of both arms control and US-Soviet detente in the early Eighties.

On a personal level, this proud, republican lawyer developed close personal and diplomatic ties with statesmen like Michael Manley of Jamaica and Lee Kuan Yew of Singapore, both of whom became strong advocates of a new deal for the debt-ravaged sub-Saharan African states.

Even after severing the last constitutional tie with the UK parliament in 1981, when he fundamentally reformed the Canadian constitution, Trudeau was happy to admit that he might never have worked with statesmen of this quality without Canada's place in the Commonwealth. There is much for Ireland to ponder in his career, and there is in the career of many other Commonwealth leaders.

The recent Irish Times letter also suggested that membership would be "be welcomed by the unionist community in Northern Ireland as a significant gesture of reconciliation. It would add to the collaborative framework established by the Belfast and St Andrew's agreements. It would demonstrate unequivocally that the Republic has finally drawn a line under the troubled history of Anglo-Irish relations that led to Ireland's self-exclusion from the Commonwealth 60 years ago."

At a time when fascistic forces like the RIRA want to drag us back to that squalid era of megaphone diplomacy and supercharged ethnic paranoia, what could be more decisive a repudiation of this hysteria than a meaningful debate on Ireland's possible contribution to the Commonwealth?[6]

---
[6] This article published in the *Irish Independent*, 29th March 2009.

WHY DID IRELAND LEAVE THE COMMONWEALTH?

BY ROBIN BURY

CHAIRMAN OF THE REFORM GROUP

The Reform Group has done some research on why the Coalition government decided to take Ireland out of the British Commonwealth in 1948. The research is based on John B O'Brien's article *'Ireland's Departure from the British Commonwealth'* in the Round Table 1988, a chapter from by MacDermott in a study of *Clann na Poblachta* and *Australia and Ireland's departure from the Commonwealth: A Reassessment* by Frank Bongiorno.

The facts seem to be as follows:

Basically, the Coalition government (Fine Gael and Clann na Poblachta) wanted to leave the Commonwealth FOR GOOD and made this quite clear to the British government in 1948 (Attlee). In fact, Dublin insisted when talking to London at that time, that they had left the Commonwealth in 1936 and they did not attend any meetings between 1936 and 1948. However, they bungled the repeal of the External Relations Act (ERA) as they did not think through the implications for Ireland north and south, particularly the enormous legal consequences. The British representative in Dublin, Lord Rugby, had a low opinion of Costello and thought he handled the repeal of the ERA in "a slapdash and amateur fashion".

When they announced they were going to repeal the ERA, they were told by the British government that there was no alternative but to treat them like any other foreign country, which meant that movement of citizens would be restricted and irreparable damage would be done to Irish trade and business with Britain. Incredibly, none of the implications of becoming a republic and leaving the Commonwealth were thought through by Costello, MacBride and the cabinet. They were, in effect, shooting their own country in the heart. And why? In MacDermott's rich metaphorical words:

"This was a two pronged robbery, aimed as much at deValera as at MacBride, for in donning the natty nationalist rain-gear of de Valera, and in stealing the republican raiment of the bathing MacBride, Costello did not merely appropriate their garments, but also enabled Fine Gael to reclaim their nationalist ancestry and heritage, and to lay claim to a portion - their portion - of the national iconography and the symbols of national identity, thereby shedding their unfortunate démodé allegiance to the Commonwealth".

All hell broke out. The initial stance of Attlee and Lord Jowitt, the Lord Chancellor, was not to be conciliatory but Dr H.V.Evatt, the Australian Deputy PM, intervened (for obscure reasons, see below) and eventually prevailed on Attlee as well as the Canadian PM, MacKenzie King, and the Canadian Secretary of State for foreign affairs, Lester Pearson (the Canadian cabinet was not supportive of the

Irish stand) and on the Australian PM, Chifley, plus New Zealand PM Peter Fraser, not to treat the Free State like a foreign country when it left the Commonwealth. Attlee and Jowitt gave way so the new ROI emerged with the same status in effect as a Commonwealth country, despite the fact that Costello and McBride were adamant that Ireland had left the Commonwealth. So far from the Free State being asked to leave the Commonwealth, great efforts were made to keep it in the Commonwealth by the big hitter members, and by the Queen Mother, to no avail. In fact, Costello, under pressure, promised he would look at returning later on but quickly forget about it when he got back to Dublin.

As far as Northern Ireland was concerned, the result was ironical and very telling. The British Ireland Bill was introduced which copper fastened the Ulster Unionists to Great Britain. This Bill would not have been introduced had the Coalition decided to keep the ERA so was brought on because of what Costello did. "If there was any doubt before the repeal of the ERA about the survival of Northern Ireland as a separate entity, there were none afterwards. It was the tactics used rather than the repeal itself which brought that about", as O'Brien puts it. MacBride's vision of a united Ireland had been "severely dented". He was very fortunate to retain Ireland's previous advantages. The dreaded Brits were accommodating the Irish as Ireland would have suffered irreparable damage to its trade and restrictions on the movement of citizens..."a policy decision had been made without regard to its consequences", as O'Brien put it.

As for Dr H.V. Evatt, the Australian Deputy PM "motives are as obscure as Costello's. He had no previous involvement in Irish internal affairs; he was not of Irish extraction and he had no instructions from Canberra, but he was destined to play a pivotal part in the crisis" according to O'Brien. Chifley, the Australian PM. "was not unduly concerned about the Irish vote in Victoria and Evatt himself, being an MP for a Sydney constituency, had little to fear personally from the Irish in Victoria, whose numbers anyway were declining. Of possibly greater importance for Evatt was his concern for world peace-keeping bodies - he had been largely instrumental in designing the Charter for the United Nations, and in 1948 he was President of that body. He was equally committed to the British Commonwealth as a vehicle for the preservation of peace and the democratic way of life in the world and was loath to see it being undermined or fragmented, especially as, in his view, Ireland was as much a mother country as Britain". Dr Evatt was "extremely indignant" at Costello's announcement. It therefore came as a great shock to the British when Dr Evatt decided to champion the Irish cause". The Canadian cabinet was "very cold towards Eire" and the New Zealand cabinet was "also quite tepid in its response".

In his essay H.V.Evatt. *'Australia and Ireland's departure from the Commonwealth: A Reassessment'* Frank Bongiorno argues that Evatt was keen 'to cultivate the Australian hierarchy' and he tried to win over Archbishop Mannix of Melbourne, calling on him frequently. Mannix was a supporter of advanced Irish nationalism, even of the extremists of 1916. Bongiorno states that Evatt was not trusted in the Labour cabinet and caucas and was driven by personal ambition. He was a Protestant but had been educated in Dublin. He hoped one day to become Prime Minister of the Labour government.

At a meeting at Chequers on 17th Oct 1948 the Irish "weakly hinted" that they might consider rejoining the Commonwealth at a later stage. On returning to Dublin they promptly dropped the idea and never raised it again. They refused to match like for like on reciprocal privileges for the Irish and Commonwealth citizens in the other person's country. The British government "placed Commonwealth solidarity before the inevitable hostile reaction to the Eire settlement". Irish votes in England were not discussed nor were a factor of any major consideration by the British government, according to O'Brien. Ireland was obdurate "in refusing to make any concession whatsoever. Britain was determined to have Irish citizens treated as aliens and to withdraw all preferences for Eire under the most favoured nation clauses of trade treaties", but Evatt would not endorse this policy partly because "Eire was covered by Sections 2 and 3 of the British nationality Act so that the UK would have to repeal these two sections".

MacBride and MacGilligan, Ireland's Minister of Finance, representing Costello, held to their position and insisted that Ireland had not been a member of the Commonwealth since 1936 and had no intention of becoming one now.

"The Irish citizens enjoyed the franchise in the UK and other Commonwealth countries; the same was not true for UK and Commonwealth citizens in Ireland". At the end of the negotiations, "Ireland was now in the Commonwealth without being in it." The Sydney Sunday Sun described it as "so typically Irish that perhaps a solution should best be left to the Irish. No other people could hope to understand it". "It achieved the immediate objective of breaking the link with the Crown" which "suited the Irish". Later on, "subsequent special ad hoc arrangements for Eire's attendance as observers were not ruled out" but in fact did not happen.

CEIST AN CHOMHLATHAIS

Le Peadar Cassidy

Retired civil servant

Tionóladh cruinniú maidir leis an Chomhlathas in Óstán Camden, Baile Átha Cliath, ar an 28ú Márta seo caite. Díospóireacht bhríomhar spreagúil a bhí ann le cainteoirí i bhfabhar is i gcoinne an rúin: As Ireland approaches the 60th anniversary of the declaration of the Republic, is it time to reconsider the country's membership of the Commonwealth?

Roy Garland, colúnaí leis an Irish News agus gníomhaí síochána, a bhí sa chathaoir agus is iad na cainteoirí a bhí ar an ardán ná an Dr Amitav Banerji, Cúrsaí Polaitíochta, Rúnaíocht an Chomhlathais, Londain; an Dr Martin Mansergh, Aire Stáit, An Roinn Airgeadais; agus John Waters, údar agus colúnaí leis an Irish Times.

Thug an Dr Banerji léargas ar stair an Chomhlathais agus ar an fhorbairt a tháinig air o 1949 i leith. Léirigh sé go soiléir nach mar a gcéanna é anois agus go bhfuil 52 tír ann anois, 32 poblacht ina measc, ina mbaill den Chomhlathas. Mhaígh sé fosta go bhfuil an bhéim i gcónaí ar an chóras daonlathach, neamhspleáchas dlíthiúil agus ar chearta daonna do chách.

Luaigh an Dr. Mansergh a athair féin, Nicholas Mansergh, Ollamh le cúrsaí Chomhlathais in Ollscoil Oxford idir 1953 agus 1969. Ba shuimiúil, a dúirt sé, go raibh díomá ar De Valera, ar F.H, Boland, Gnóthaí Eachtracha, is ar a athair faoin scoilt sa bhliain 1949. Dar leis nach bhfuil aon seans go n-osclófar an cheist sa tír seo go luath.

Labhair John Waters go neamhbhalbh i gcoinne an rúin. Mhaígh sé gur fhulaing a mhuintir faoi Choilíniú na Breataine agus gur scriosadh ár dteanga dúchais lena linn freisin. Is mór leis, a dúirt sé, litríocht na Breataine ach anois measann sé gur cuid den saol atá thart an Comhlathas is gach rud a bhaineann leis.

Mhol toscaire as Málta ón urlár nach cóir bheith ag breathnú siar i gcónaí ach féachaint chun leas na tíre sa todhchaí.

Is é an t-eagras an 'Reform Movement' a bhí taobh thiar den chruinniú, grúpa daoine atá fabharach do pholasaí na Poblachta a leathnú gur féidir leis an Phoblacht dul i bpáirt le tíortha an Chomhlathais in athuair. Ábhar conspóideach, achrannach le cuid mhór daoine le fada an lá, maireann sé ina cnámh spairne go fóill. Tá an scéal á phlé i láthair na huaire ar an raidió, ar na páipéir agus ar an idirlíon, ar ndóigh. Taobh amuigh den 'Alliance' agus na Dílseoirí, níl aon chomhartha ann go nglacfadh aon pháirtí leis an mholadh mar pholasaí.[7]

---

[7] This article was published in the April issue of 'An tUltach' (The Ulsterman), a monthly produced by Comhdháil Uladh, an associate of the Gaelic League.

FOR BETTER OR WORSE

BY MARTIN MANSERGH TD

MINISTER OF STATE AT THE DEPARTMENT OF FINANCE AND THE ARTS

Speech delivered at the 'Ireland and Commonwealth Conference' at Camden Court Hotel, Dublin, 28th March 2009.

I would like to thank the Reform Movement for their invitation to address this subject, in which I have more a personal than a political interest. The Commonwealth was a subject in which my father the historian Nicholas Mansergh (1910-91), born and brought up in Tipperary, held a professional chair in Cambridge named after Jan Smuts between 1953 and 1969, and about which he wrote extensively. Having been involved myself since 1981 as a civil servant and advisor on Northern

Ireland policy and what used to be called Anglo-Irish relations, now British-Irish relations, I have a fair knowledge of the rare occasions on which the subject was brought up, and am also in some position to form a political assessment of the matter.

I do not intend, nor is it my function, to make policy pronouncements on this subject. I will confine myself to analysis, historical and political, and explain why I do not regard the subject of Ireland's membership of the Commonwealth as a live issue, or likely to become one, as far as this State is concerned. I appreciate that it would be the intention of this Conference to try and alter that, but, to succeed, it would be necessary to enlist the support of one or more political parties and of course of public opinion at large.

One of the most resonant rebukes was delivered by Mikhail Gorbachev in the early autumn of 1989 to the politburo of the German Democratic Republic, which was celebrating the 40th anniversary of its foundation: 'History punishes those who move too late.' Within two months, the Berlin wall had fallen, and within a year the GDR itself was gone, with a united Germany taking its place.

There are several examples in our own history of the same phenomenon criticised by Gorbachev. If Catholic Emancipation had accompanied the Union, as Pitt intended, the Union would have been associated from the beginning with reform. If Home Rule had been accepted, in effect as an historic compromise between Unionism and Nationalism in the island as a whole, our historical development could have been far more benign, whether or not it had subsequently developed into full dominion status. 'What fools we were not to have accepted Gladstone's Home Rule Bill. The Empire would not have had the Free State giving us so much trouble and pulling us to pieces,' George V told his Prime Minister Ramsay McDonald in 1930. In 1998, David Trimble avoided the mistake of earlier Unionist leaders, when he negotiated and accepted the Good Friday Agreement.

The Commonwealth, the subject of today's conference, is, in my opinion, another prime example of history punishing movement that came too late. Without going too much into the history, I would like to outline, why Ireland's experience with the Commonwealth, up until it left in 1949, was an unhappy one.

The very name had associations with the mid-17th century Commonwealth period, and the first person to use it was Lord Rosebery, former Liberal Prime Minster, who published a book in 1900 called Oliver Cromwell: A Eulogy and an Appreciation. Lionel Curtis, in many ways the ideologue of the Commonwealth, who worked for the British delegation during the Treaty negotiations, explained that 'hunting about for a good Saxon word... I naturally hit on the word Commonwealth'.

Of far more significance is the fact that British insistence on no more than dominion status in the Treaty negotiations, as opposed to a Republic externally associated with the Commonwealth, led to a rupture within the independence movement over the Treaty, subsequently to civil war, particularly when Churchill, Curtis and others adamantly rejected the draft constitution agreed between de Valera and Collins in May 1922, from which explicit reference to the crown had been removed.

In the 1920s, the Irish Free State played an important role in the evolution of the British Commonwealth of Nations into a partnership of equals. The majority of people never warmed to imposed Dominion status, though that was of course strongly valued in particular by the ex-unionist community. After the change of government and the advent of de Valera in 1932, the State did attend the Ottawa Conference. But Commonwealth membership was clouded over by the economic war and British resistance to dismantling the Treaty, which, in their view, took precedence over Ireland's right to enjoy subsequent developments in Commonwealth status in 1926 and 1931.

Post-abdication, a form of external association was achieved by the adoption of a constitution that was internally republican, but retained a residual diplomatic function for the king. Pressures on neutral Ireland during the war came about, because Churchill in particular did not accept its right to make its own decisions. The Commonwealth countries in contrast did participate in the war. Post-war, the ambiguous nature of the State, summed up by the jibe of 'dictionary republic', and also its status in relation to the Commonwealth, lead to a clear break in April 1949, the same month as India declared a Republic and remained. There were those at the time, de Valera, F H Boland in External Affairs, and indeed my father, who were critical both of the decision of the John A Costello-led First Interparty Government and the abrupt way in which it came about.

The criticism was that it burnt bridges with the North, that de Valera had tried to hold open, and also that the older Dominions with substantial populations of Irish extraction had been good friends to Ireland, often more so than Britain. The small Protestant minority in the South certainly took it badly, and in some cases transferred their party preference. I can remember the Rector of Tipperary continuing to pray in Church for the Queen as Head of the Commonwealth into the early 1960s. One serious political consequence of the final break was the proclamation of the British guarantee to the Parliament at Stormont, which appeared to solidify partition.

Over the following 25 years, the Commonwealth occasionally surfaced with the 1957 Cardinal d'Alton unity initiative, in Lemass' 1959 Oxford Union speech, and in occasional speeches of Jack Lynch, which indicated that Ireland would be prepared to reconsider Commonwealth membership in the context of bringing about a united Ireland. There have only been very isolated instances, where re-entry of this State outside of unity has been advocated by any Government figure.

The world has moved on in the past 60 years. The Commonwealth, once decolonisation was complete, became of arguably fairly marginal significance even to British Governments and impatient Prime Ministers, the monarch of course having a stronger attachment. Even for Britain, the European Union is a much more important organisation.

Commonwealth membership for the Republic, if occasionally raised, was never pressed by unionists in political negotiations. How far unionists identify with the modern Commonwealth is a moot point, but they would not have desired to raise expectation or put any extra pressure on themselves as a result of such a change. If it had happened, they would have been more likely to suggest that it be viewed as a move towards Irish rapprochement with the United Kingdom, rather than removing an obstacle to a united Ireland.

Ireland has a close and strong bilateral relationship with Britain, without need of any multilateral international organisation like the Commonwealth. It was put on a new footing in 1949 with the Common Travel Area, and legislation on both sides ensuring that neither would treat the other as foreign countries. Separate, yes, foreign no, something totally ignored by most unionists and nationalists alike, at least in their political discourse. The East-West relationship is symbolised through, but scarcely needs, formal British-Irish institutions, such as the British-Irish Council.

The Northern Troubles probably exacerbated resentment of a monarchical institution that was required to be Protestant, heading the Commonwealth, because of the perceived misuse of this to bolster the dominance of one section of the community in Northern Ireland. This aspect certainly provides an instant emotive objection, though there has been some tentative nibbling at the edges of this by New Labour as late as yesterday.

Far the most important factor, however, is Ireland's identity in the world. Ireland has chosen the European path, and pursued a strategy different from Britain's of seeking to be at the heart of Europe. With geographical expressions like the British Isles in continental weather forecasts, the classification by the French media of Ireland as one of the 'Anglo-Saxon' economies, Commonwealth membership would be perceived by many of our European partners, however inaccurately, as a step back, and as Ireland falling back into the British sphere of influence, which would be detrimental to our interests.

There would be, to sum up, very strong resistance on both historical and contemporary grounds to re-entry, even though republics now form a majority of Commonwealth States, and even though in general, outside of defence, countries tend to join most international organisations that they are eligible to join, provided the cost is nominal.

President Sarkozy said recently that independent nations, if they are to exercise influence, need to choose what families they belong to. He was speaking in the context of the French decision to reintegrate fully into NATO. There is a part of our psyche that still hankers after what was called at the time of the Treaty debate 'the isolated Republic'. We have decided that we belong to the European family of nations, and, of course, even if the people were to vote 'no' a second time to Lisbon, Commonwealth membership would not even begin to compensate us. David Trimble once urged us to rejoin the Commonwealth and 'the British family of nations.' It is an inaccurate description, and I very much doubt, if many Commonwealth countries, such as India or South Africa, see themselves in that light, but there is no doubt that Irish public opinion would have no argument with Trimble's description of the Commonwealth, and on that basis reject it.

Post-Good Friday Agreement, there were some tentative approaches from the then Nigerian Secretary-General of the Commonwealth. President Nelson Mandela's hosting of a Commonwealth Conference in South Africa might have been politically tempting. Taoiseach Bertie Ahern flew a kite about Partnership for Peace and the Commonwealth in a Sunday Times interview. According to what he told me, Partnership for Peace passed muster at the Fianna Fáil Parliamentary Party, but there was a negative reaction to the Commonwealth. The debate he said he would welcome never took place for lack of interest. The only other ministerial figure to mention it prior to the Agreement was Eamon O Cuiv, conscious of his grandfather's thinking, and trying to be helpful to the negotiations. Even in the context of some future negotiations on a united Ireland, I would not be confident that Commonwealth membership would be an easy or acceptable concession here, though I would hate to see unity founder on a dispute over symbols.

I see nothing on the horizon, which would persuade the public to reverse its attitude, or to see advantages in renewed membership. For better or worse, in the present state of opinion, the Commonwealth is history, as far as this State is concerned.

WHAT IF?

An RTE radio discussion entitled, "What if?" between Geoffrey Roberts Department of History, University College, Cork and Noel Dorr former ambassador, diplomat and secretary of the Department of Foreign Affairs. Chaired by Dermot Ferriter in late April 2008.

The story of the modern commonwealth began in 1926 with the Balfour Declaration. That document described the commonwealth as "a free association of equal states in no way subordinate one to another". The Statute of Westminster of 1931 formally removed any remaining legal restraints on the independence of Commonwealth states. Two countries most responsible for forcing these changes were Canada and Ireland. The Commonwealth ministers like Desmond Fitzgerald and Patrick McGilligan playing a leading role.

After Finna Fail came to power in 1932 while DeValera eroded the village crowns role in internal Irish affairs he did not take Ireland out of the Commonwealth. Ireland was the only Commonwealth country to remain neutral during the Second World War and by the end of that war the Irish relationship with the Commonwealth was almost invisible. A London Declaration of 1949 removed the word 'British' from the organisation's name and set out the constitutional formula which made it possible for the republics to retain Commonwealth membership. But the London Declaration came only eight days after Ireland announced that upon becoming a republic it would leave the Commonwealth, which it did on the 18th of April 1949 when Fine Gael's John A Costello was Taoiseach. On a trip to Canada the previous September Costello had announced his government's intention in this regard. At various stages over the last fifty years the idea of Ireland rejoining the commonwealth has been floated. What if Ireland had not left the Commonwealth in the first place, and what if it had rejoined? My guests this morning with me in the studio is Noel Dorr, former ambassador, diplomat and secretary of the Department of Foreign Affairs and in the studio in

Cork, Geoffrey Roberts from the Department of History University College, Cork. You are both very welcome.

Noel can I go to you first?

When we talk about Ireland in the context of the commonwealth other countries are often mentioned like Canada, Australia and New Zealand. I suppose the difference is that Ireland was a dominion by revolution rather than evolution, that it had been imposed on Ireland by a large extent causing a lot of strife as well. Is the real surprise that the Commonwealth connection lasted as long as it did?

Possibly, yes. I think it's also interesting to notice the thesis of Irish nationalism in the early 20s was that Ireland was a mother country where these other countries were countries of settlement. Nicholas Mansergh, who is the father of Martin Mansergh, and who is a distinguished historian of Cambridge and a great expert on the Commonwealth, sees three phases to Ireland's relationship to the Commonwealth. The three experiments he calls them. The first was the period following the Treaty, when Ireland was the Free State that it was with a dominion with status equal to Canada. Second stage, or second experiment as he calls it, followed the External Relations Act in the Constitution 1936-37 and from then on it was really closer to DeValera's original idea of external association. In fact Mansergh says, and I am quoting "during that period Eire owed no allegiance to the Crown and was not in the Irish view a member of the British Commonwealth of Nations but a state with association with it from without, which was symbolised by the King's signature to the Letters of Appointment of Irish Representatives. Now it's not clear that the Commonwealth itself accepted the idea of associate status but according to this and other things that I have read from the Irish point of view, Ireland was an associate state. Mancerg also makes a further interesting point, he describes the commonwealth as really a "super structure" on the British/Irish relationship or the Anglo Irish relationship, and he sees the relationship itself as more important than the "super structure".

Geoffrey, when you look at this whole question of allegiance to the crown, I mean it obviously carried a weight of historical baggage in Ireland, perhaps did not provide the same focus of loyalty as it did in Australia,

New Zealand and so on. Is there a tendency for us here to over-emphasise this and forget the historical links that Ireland had to the commonwealth and the Empire?

Geoffrey

I think that is probably true. The interesting thing of course is that at the moment that Ireland leaves the Commonwealth the terms of Commonwealth membership changes and the British monarch becomes a symbol of the free association of independence of states, so a period like symbolic headship of the Commonwealth. That was established because in 1949 India became a member of the Commonwealth as a republic. So it was open to Ireland in 1949 to actually do the same thing as India that is to declare itself a republic but at the same time maintain its membership of the Commonwealth. Perhaps even negotiate some kind of deal as far as the monarch's symbolic role as head of Commonwealth.

Did you get that impression that DeValera was waiting to see what happened with India and he didn't make the decision on the Commonwealth at an earlier stage in the 1930?

Noel

It's arguable. I think that the decision was taken too soon. DeValera was not in office at the time the decision was taken, it was an inter-party government and it's possible that had the decision come later, the Commonwealth would have evolved by then. India had to be accommodated in 1949. India was too important and too large from a British point of view and from the point of view of the other dominions, so an accommodation was reached but in Ireland's case the decision was taken earlier so possibly DeValera's approach might have been to wait and wait and see what the Commonwealth would have all been into. Its interesting however that the other dominions supported the Irish case at that time for a special relationship and the special relationship was embodied in the Ireland Act 1949 which interestingly had two facets that should be remembered. One is declared explicitly, that" the Republic of Ireland, though not a member of the Commonwealth, is not a foreign country" and I sometimes thought that Unionists in the North might have been told that an Act of Parliament actually said the Republic is not a foreign country. But the other one was one that I have personal experience of. I was ambassador in London for four years in the 1980s and I noted that on ceremonial occasions, lets say when a head of state was visiting, the ambassadors dressed up in morning suits and were presented one by one to the visiting Head of State and the protocol in the Foreign office always put the High Commissioners of Commonwealth countries in one room and the ambassadors in another. They would each go in, in turn, and be greeted by the Head of State. I was always told to go in with the High Commissioners, that is with the Commonwealth countries. Nobody explained this to me, and I was told while going in that they would go in first and I was to go in a little bit behind them and a little bit in front of the first of the ambassadors and I deduced for myself that that derives from precise provision in the Ireland Act 1948 which says: "The person who in the United Kingdom is the chief representative of the Republic of Ireland or the government of Ireland shall, whatever the style of his office, have the same privileges and exemptions as to taxations and otherwise, as the High Commissioners."

So there was a relic of something there that no-one had told me about but I think that that is the correct assumption that that was what was happening.

Geoffrey

Young Members of the Commonwealth were keen that Ireland's departure from the Commonwealth did not actually damage Ireland's relationships with members of the Commonwealth, which is why they worked very had to moderate the British response to Ireland's departure from the Commonwealth, which, initially, was a very hard line response which was, if Ireland was leaving the Commonwealth then we were treated like a foreign country. The other countries hoped of course that Ireland would rejoin the Commonwealth perhaps within a short period of time.

Can I just make a point about DeValera; DeValera of course was on record of being in favour of continuing membership of the Commonwealth because he saw it as a bridge to the Northern Unionists. In a way this is the main point about Irish departure from the Commonwealth, it actually burnt that bridge and that was an important bridge.

But here were other individuals like Cardinal Dalton who made the same point. Sean Lemass addressed this issue as well when he addressed the Oxford Union in 1959 and we have a clip here of that speech.

"Rising out of the one statement I have made I think I should say that we recognise, we accept, that in any conference held to negotiate a settlement of this issue the question of the relationship between a reunited Ireland and the Commonwealth would certainly be an important item on the Agenda, that our goal in the reunification of Ireland by agreement, and I am not pretending that we can expect, or that we are expecting speedy results. The barriers of fear and suspicion in the minds of the partitionists are too strong to be demolished quickly. For that reason, our aim is to develop contacts which will tend to build goodwill. We hope to proceed in that way step by step to a new situation to which a reappraisal of the whole situation can be undertaken unhampered by prejudice.

That was Sean Lemass speaking at the Oxford Union in 1959. Jeffrey, do you think if Ireland had stayed in the Commonwealth that some of those issues would have been easier to deal with?

Geoffrey

I do. I think it would have maintained the bridge with the Northern Unionists and I think it would have helped moderate Unionists domination of Northern Ireland. I think perhaps it would have led to an earlier reconstruction of North/South relations like the reconstruction that took place with LeMass and Terence O'Neill in the mid 1960s and perhaps we wouldn't have had thirty years of troubles had Ireland remained in the Commonwealth.

Is that an analysis you would go along with Noel?

Noel

I would like to think it would have happened but I don't think it would. I think Sean Lemass's approach was admirable but remember that from the Treaty onwards, Ireland was in the Commonwealth until 1936/1937. Arguably from then until 1948 it was associated with the Commonwealth and I suppose each of those was a link that one might hope would be useful but it didn't work out. I think myself that the idea of joining the Commonwealth, which would have been useful, it would have been a framework of contacts abroad for us and all sorts of things at a time when we were perhaps a bit cut off after the neutrality of the war and all that. But looking at it in relation to the problems of this island it seems to me to go with an older analysis. The nationalist analysis which saw it as a matter of persuading the Unionists by relatively modest concessions, and getting the British to help and that some other natural road would lead to a united Ireland. I think what has brought the current settlement is a much more sophisticated analysis which began in the early 1970s which looks at aspects intrinsic to Northern Ireland, to two communities, one potential minority, the other a natural minority, in contention over the unsolved aspects of the old Irish problem with the perhaps wrong type of structure in Stormont for a divided community and the focus now has been on consent, on partnership, on an Irish dimension which is intrinsic to the North and not simply a claim by the South on the North. Also I think, and this is the most important thing, on getting a process of reconciliation underway and letting each step decide the next step, not trying to decide the long term future. Now if the Commonwealth would help in that, great. Some Irish people would find it a little emotionally difficult to accept. It would help greatly but I don't think it would be sufficient, or that it would have been sufficient until now at least, to persuade Unionists and perhaps it was too simplistic on nationalism to think it might have been.

Geoffrey

I think I would say in response to that that perhaps the Peace Process in a broad sense could have actually started in the 1950s/1960s and that Ireland's continued membership of the Commonwealth might have provided a useful framework to encourage that sort of development but as it was we know that historically it made things a lot worse. It reinforced partition; it added to the polarisation of identities, it gave all kinds of excuses to the Northern Unionists to actually exercise longevity in Northern Ireland in a particular way. I mean you have to remember what was the Union response to Ireland's departure from the Commonwealth? Basil Brooke, the Northern Ireland Prime Minster, made a speech in which he says "Ireland's departure from the Commonwealth shows that there are two different communities in Ireland." In fact he called a general election on the back of this Irish decision and the election issue was Northern Ireland's connection to Britain. The subsequent negotiations to do with the Ireland Act of

1949 where Britain is renegotiating its relationship with the Republic of Ireland by that time, the Unionists take the opportunity to establish legislative veto over any change in the Constitution of arrangements as far as Northern Ireland is concerned. Now those developments are absolutely critical to the subsequent development of North/South relations and I think they do actually lead, not directly, but quite significantly, to the problems that occur.

Noel

Geoffrey may be right, it's a matter of judgement and I prefer to bow to him as a historian! I would point out that we were in the Commonwealth, or connected with it for twenty six years, and since 1973 we have been members of the EU along with the UK and therefore Northern Ireland. Now perhaps those contacts have helped in relations between the two governments. My only point was that not to object to the concept, if it would help it would be great and at any time I would have taken that view and there are others who thought it might have helped and maybe Geoffrey is right. My feeling is that the resistance of the Unionists to unity was deeper than we accepted or realised on the part of Irish nationalism and it is to the extent that we have come to realise that and to try to live with it and accommodate to it and work with them in partnership.

It's also a question of the geography. I mean Ireland was Britain's neighbour either way they were going to have fairly close contacts as a result of geography.

Noel

Yes you get back to Manserghs point that the Commonwealth for Ireland as distinct from the other dominions or for the Free State, or for the Irish Republic, was a kind of super structure over the relationship which had to be intense in any event. It was deep, it was turbulent, it was long, historical, it was emotional physiologically, and every other way, and there was a centrifugal impulse on the part of Irish nationalism up to relatively recently. Now joining the EU has helped in that it's course today. It's very, very different but his point was that the relationship is deep whatever kind of super structure you put on it. The Commonwealth for Ireland, and I am not talking about the other dominions, was an attempt to accommodate it, but it was a super structure and even if the Commonwealth was removed the relationship continued. But of course Commonwealth membership would have been helpful to Irish ministers. It would have given them an opening to the world. It would have made contacts possible and indeed Jeffrey Powell, the former Foreign Secretary in Britain, always emphasised the importance of the membership of both countries in so to speak lubricating the relationship between ministers. They met regularly in Brussels in a way that was no longer the kind of occasional and rather dramatic meetings that you had before that. Maybe the Commonwealth would have helped in that.

Geoffrey, another thing that emerged in the 1950s and the 1960s was this question of deconalisation. Had Ireland been in the Commonwealth would they have been in a position to do more about that given their own experiences? I mean people like Frank Aiken, who was Minister of External Affairs used to say "We stand unequivocally for the swift and orderly ending of colonial rule." Some of those who were involved in the Commonwealth of course afterwards made the point that they had come through that process of decolonisation and Ireland had not much experience of it.

Geoffrey

I think that is a very important point because the historical point at which Ireland leaves the Commonwealth, the Commonwealth is actually on the verge of a fundamental transformation of its character rising out of the dismantlement of the British Empire in the Third World and the whole process of decolonisation. The Commonwealth is very much part of that process of decolonisation and in fact acts as a bridge to world affairs for the newly independent countries of the former British Empire. The point is of course in the 1920s and the 1930s the Commonwealth played the same role for Ireland in world affairs as being a very important bridge to world affairs for the Irish Free State. So the same thing happens for the newly independent countries of the 50s and 60s and of course the Irish experience would have been a very important part of that process. I think Ireland could have made an important contribution to the transformation of the Commonwealth, including the enhancement of its role in the process.

I suppose a lot of people would have argued that they had the United Nations as a firm to articulate those kind of things.

Geoffrey

Ireland did not become a member of the United Nations until 1955 of course. It's not a question of either or, it's obvious that the UN is critical to decolonisation. I think maybe the Commonwealth is more important than we think and actually the Irish, rather than with the Commonwealth, would have been much more influential than the role it was able to play in the UN. So it took quiet a long time for Ireland to establish itself with the UN.

Noel

I think that, let me be quite clear, I think being in the Commonwealth would have held it in both sides and to that extent I accept that there would have been emotional problems here in Ireland, I have said that already, but as to the United Nations, Ireland joined the United Nations in 1955 and the real decolonisation took place late in the 50s and through the 60s. That was the period that Frank Aiken, who was regarded with great respect at the time, he was someone who himself had fought for independence, he was able to point out that back as far as 1913/1914 he had joined the Nationalist Movement and that he was fighting for independence but now he urged these countries that there was now an organisation in the United Nations which provided the framework for them and therefore they didn't need to find the peaceful means so to speak. He was quite an influential figure in that regard and I think that the existence of the United Nations, it's a historic fact that it is not often looked at, it eased the whole transition which took place especially in the second half of the twentieth century, from a world of colonies and empires to a world of sovereign independent states. It was the framework into which the newly independent states aspired to join. The first thing you did when you became independent was to apply to join the United Nations. It was a symbol of independence and also in a sense a guarantee of independence. Now the Commonwealth within the United Nations had a useful role and I am not denying that, but the United Nations it seems to me was the more important. You had a charter laid down and agreed and we have turned it into an international constitution for international society.

There is also the question of Ireland and the Commonwealth emerging in the 1980s and we have a news report here from 1985.

"The official Unionist leader, Mr James Molyneaux, has claimed that civil servants at the British and Irish governments have been talking about the possibility of the Republic rejoining the British Commonwealth. He said the talks had been going on for several months and the programme of Anglo Irish studies had also been stepped up. Mr Molyneaux made his claims after being asked about a report in the Belfast News letter this morning that Dr. Fitzgerald was hinting at the move in a paper about to be presented to the New Ireland Forum. Mr. Molyneaux said that he did not think it had anything to do with the Forum but he said he thought it would be a welcome step as long as the Dublin government accepted that it didn't give them any right to medal in Northern Ireland affairs. He said he thought that the government in the South now recognised they have lost out economically by isolating themselves from what he called "the natural unit of the British Isles."

That was Charles Mitchell reading the news in 1985. You were very closely involved in Northern Anglo discussions at that stage did you have any idea of this?

Noel

No. I was Irish ambassador in London during the Irish Anglo negotiations which led to the Agreement of 1985, the two Prime Ministers Garret Fitzgerald and Margaret Thatcher, signed the Agreement if you remember in November 1985. Jim Molyneaux I don't think had told the right end of it there. Of course there was talk in general in public, there was nothing secret about it, but it was not in issue in any event in any of these negotiations. I am sorry to say that Enoch Powell at the time had huge conspiracy theories also and I don't know how far Jim Molyneaux went along with some of that but it wasn't a real issue that I recall at that time. It was something that was talked about speculatively but there is no big conspiracy and it wasn't a serious subject that I recall. In any event at that time in Irish Anglo negotiations just because the relationship was intense, far more intense that the Commonwealth would have produced. The Anglo Irish Agreement did provide a good resolution of the issues between Irish ministers. It didn't as far as the communities in the North were concerned of course, but it was a more intense relationship than membership of the Commonwealth would have produced. If it helped the Unionists fine, but it wasn't talked about seriously.

Was it inevitable Geoffrey that it would emerge again in the context of the Peace Process?

Geoffrey

I think so, yes. Interesting point. I made the point earlier that the Unionists actually welcomed Ireland's departure from the Commonwealth 1n 1948/49 and they were glad Ireland remained outside the Commonwealth in the 50s ,60s and 70s as they felt it was best from their point of view and their relationship with Britain. Of course in the context of the Peace Process and negotiations linked to the Good Friday Agreement, and everything that has happened since, Unionists attitudes have changed. Now they are very much in favour, I think anyway, of Irish membership of the Commonwealth and they would see this as a hugely symbolic gesture that the Republic could have made as a kind of recognition of their identity and their history and of their tradition.

Does it not raise the question, and Noel raised it earlier, about the emotional reaction in Ireland. If you were to ask various people the straight question if they wanted to rejoin the Commonwealth, chances are the majority would say no.

My sense wouldn't be that. My sense would be that most people would accept that position of rejoining the Commonwealth if there was political leadership. If the Irish political elite decided that that was what they wanted to do and they made the case I think that most Irish people would be comfortable with the renewal of Ireland's relationship with the Commonwealth which after all is no longer the British Empire. The Commonwealth today is very very different.

And most of the members are republics. (32)

Absolutely.

Noel

I can say that I went in May 1980 as an official for Foreign Affairs with the Taoiseach Charles Haughey at his first meeting with Mrs. Thatcher and at that time the big phrase that he had introduced and again which was important in Anglo Irish relations, was the totality of relations between these islands, That was the framework in which to deal with the legacy problem of Northern Ireland. He had a private meeting with Mrs. Thatcher and he came out to the Press Conference and it was really full of the possibilities that lay ahead. The relationship soured later as one knows but at that time it was full of the possibilities but one of the journalists asked him "what about joining the Commonwealth?" and he immediately said "no". It was a kind of emotional reaction which was typical of the time. I would venture to say that I had retired by the time of the Good Friday Agreement in 1998, but it would seem to me that if it was really a matter that Unionist attach great importance to it, the Irish side would have been willing to go along with it at that time. There was such an openness and so many things were accepted in that Agreement and we got rid of Articles 2 and 3 and so on. Iif it had really counted I think it would have been one of the elements in that Agreement. I wouldn't be opposed to it at all but I am just trying to emphasise it wouldn't have done the trick.

Ok I am afraid we are going to have to leave it there for this morning. Thanks to Geoffrey Roberts in Cork and to Noel Dorr here in the studio.

END

WESTMINSTER HALL COMMONWEALTH DEBATE

By Andrew MacKinlay MP

On 24th June 2007, Andrew MacKinlay, Labour MP for Thurrock initiated a debate on Ireland's membership of the Commonwealth with the following speech.

I am pleased to initiate this debate on Ireland's membership of the Commonwealth—a business that stands deferred since April 1949. As I hope to demonstrate in the next few minutes, ministerial responsibility has been involved. You, Mr. Hood, and I are proud of the Commonwealth, which has 53 sovereign, independent member states, only 16 of which have Queen Elizabeth II as head of state. I shall refer to that again, because it is important to place on the record that the overwhelming majority of Commonwealth members are republics.

I am proud of the fact that the Commonwealth is an informal, mutually owned organisation that does an awful lot of good around the world—somewhat silently, but to the tremendous benefit of millions of people. Each Commonwealth country is responsible for its own policies, but they all work together in consultation and co-operation in the interests of their people. They try to reduce conflict and are involved in conflict prevention and bringing peace to the world.

The Commonwealth's strength is in its diversity and geographical extent—rich and poor, developed and undeveloped, north and south. Commonwealth countries' common factors include a common language, in many cases, as well as history and democratic values. Such values are the cornerstone of the Commonwealth and are enshrined in the Singapore declaration of Commonwealth principles, made in 1971 and reiterated at Harare in 1991.

The Commonwealth works closely with and in the spirit of the United Nations charter. Many organisations are related to Commonwealth agencies, including the Commonwealth Development Corporation and the scientific and education organisations. Many of us are proud of what is probably the second biggest single festival of sport—the Commonwealth games, which are very important to all the participants and countries involved.

That is the background to the Commonwealth of which you and I are very proud, Mr. Hood. However, in my mind's eye, each time there is a Commonwealth Heads of Government meeting, or CHOGM, there is an empty chair, in front of which is a notice bearing the words "Republic of Ireland". Why do I use the empty-chair analogy? To me, an empty chair indicates the temporary absence of an occupant who will return, or that the attendance of the person for whom the chair is designated has been delayed.

I use the analogy because historians, both in the Republic of Ireland and here, say—erroneously, in my view—that Ireland left the Commonwealth when Taoiseach John Costello decided in August 1948 to repeal the Executive

Authority (External Relations) Act 1936 and inaugurate the Republic of Ireland on Easter Monday 1949.

However, I think that the historians are wrong: at that time, the Commonwealth, to the extent that it existed, was nothing like the Commonwealth of today. Its only sovereign, independent states in April 1949 were Canada, Australia, New Zealand and South Africa, apart from Ireland. The Commonwealth of the time bore no relationship to that of today. There is also the backdrop: at the time, all but Eire had been involved in what was then the recent second world war. Relations between not only Ireland and the United Kingdom, but those other states were still somewhat fraught—something epitomised by the exchanges of Winston Churchill and Eamon De Valera in their two great broadcasts of May 1945.

However, things have moved on, and I raise this matter today in that spirit. It is also important to remember that, paradoxically, some of the great Irish statesmen have contributed to the modern Commonwealth. One is Eamon De Valera, who in 1921 came up with the concept of external association. At the time, the British Government could not get their heads around the idea that a state could be associated with those other states, with their historic ties and traditions, and yet be a republic. Valera's document No. 2 in the treaty negotiations of 1921 was spurned and rejected.

However, it came alive again five days after the Republic of Ireland was inaugurated by Taoiseach Costello in April 1949, because on 22, 25 and 26 April that year, the Prime Ministers of the remaining countries of what was then called the Commonwealth agreed that in 1950 Pandit Nehru could bring his newly independent India into the Commonwealth as its first republic.

De Valera's concept of external association was adopted, but unfortunately those dealing with relations with Ireland could not get their heads around the idea that that formulation for India should have been triggered for Ireland in 1948-49. The rest is history; as I have said, the majority of Commonwealth countries take advantage of the concept and are republics within the Commonwealth.

I have mentioned Eamon De Valera, but his adversaries in the Irish domestic situation also contributed greatly to the modern Commonwealth. I refer particularly to Desmond

Fitzgerald—father of Garret Fitzgerald—Kevin O'Higgins and Patrick McGilligan. In the dominion conferences of the '20s and '30s—after the creation of the Irish Free State and with the support of W.T. Cosgrave, the Free State Premier—those men tried to stretch the envelope of their independence and enthusiastically interested the other countries in doing so.

The Anglo-Irish treaty of 1921 stated that the Irish Free State would have the same status as Canada's. That was seized by the plenipotentiaries who signed that treaty, but they went on to try to increase and build on it. They argued and persuaded Canada and Australia to seek greater independence; that was reflected in legislation such as the Royal and Parliamentary Titles Act 1927. However, the culmination was the Statute of Westminster 1931, which is still the cornerstone of the independence of Canada, Australia, New Zealand and many other countries.

When Eamon De Valera came into office in 1932, he was able to abolish the oath. On the occasion of the abdication, he was able to alter the Irish Free State's head of state position—he did away with the post of Governor-General, created the office of President, and moved things on a ratchet towards a republic, which he desired and for which he had a mandate. He also introduced the Executive Authority (External Relations) Act 1936, which reduced the role of the monarch to a residual one, by which diplomatic representation was notionally done through the King and the signing of treaties. In every other respect, Ireland had moved to being a republic, although it was not declared as such.

I have given that history because when we come to 1948-49 there was the apparent breach that I mentioned. As I said, the formula extended to Pandit Nehru was unfortunately not extended to, offered to or taken up by Ireland, although in retrospect it should have been. I do not think that it is too late for that to happen.

It is also interesting that Clement Attlee was somewhat exercised by the Taoiseach Costello declaration. However, he had the good counsel of the Canadian External Affairs Minister, the great Lester Pearson, and that of Prime Ministers Chifley of Australia and Fraser of New Zealand. My predecessor, the late, great Hugh Delargy, MP for Thurrock, helped persuade the British Government to pass the Ireland Act 1949, which decided not to treat Irish men and women as aliens, but to give them special status, which they enjoy today. I should say in parenthesis that as a consequence, many Members of this House of Commons hold Irish citizenship or are entitled to; some Ministers do, I think.

A special relationship was created, anyway, but the terminology was not such that that Ireland was in the Commonwealth and, as I have said, that was followed by non-attendance at Commonwealth councils, at CHOGM and so on, which I regret. It should have been, as the spirit was that the franchise was as available to people of the Republic of Ireland as it was to citizens of the United Kingdom.

By the mid-1950s, Ireland had joined the United Nations under External Affairs Minister Frank Aiken and since then it has not only been a great player in the United Nations but has been great friends of the Secretary-General, particularly using its small but highly skilled armed forces in the delicate matter of peace operations. It has contributed enormously to that, and I mention it because part of the role of the Commonwealth is peace, conflict prevention, keeping potential adversaries apart and trying to keep safety.

Of course, Ireland has had a distinguished role in the European Union. It has held the presidency very successfully on a number of occasions. Ireland has a small population, but with great professionalism it punches above its weight in the United Nations, the European Union and many other councils. The missing element in my view, to our disadvantage, is its lack of membership of the Commonwealth.

The Commonwealth is run by a small secretariat. It is not the British Commonwealth, but the Commonwealth—it has not been the British Commonwealth for decades. Its secretary-general has never been drawn from the United Kingdom: the present one is a former and distinguished Foreign Minister of New Zealand. I hope and think that one day the natural supply for the role of secretary-general would be professional diplomats from the Irish Republic or even a retired Taoiseach who has done so much to bring peace in our islands and throughout the world.

What do I want from the debate? I trust that it will not be seen as presumptuous, but I hope that the United Kingdom branch of the Commonwealth Parliamentary Association might reflect on what I have said and extend invitations to members of the Oireachtas to any of its future conferences. It might also raise the issue in the international conference of the CPA. I hope that both the secretary-general of the CPA and the secretary-general of the Commonwealth, Don McKinnon, will also take on board some of my remarks.

I hope that the high commissioners in London of the Commonwealth countries, particularly those of Australia, Canada and New Zealand, because of their historic role and because so many of their fellow countrymen and women are part of the Irish diaspora—the Irish diaspora are in every corner of the Commonwealth, playing a full part in business commerce and public life—will reflect on what I have said. I hope that the Irish embassy in London will reflect on what I have said. I hope that it will not be too presumptuous to ask the Minister if—if I can persuade him that I have a case— to refer the matter to our Prime Minister. We are in a new era of relationships. I do not say that this should come about because of the Good Friday agreement and the success of 8 May this year, with the new dispensation for north and south, Catholic and Protestant, republican and Unionist. The time is right for Ireland to take its place in the club in which it has not taken up its seat.

This case needs to be remedied. I hope that those countries that are not independent sovereign states in the Commonwealth, such as our friends in the Isle of Man, might discuss the matter in their legislatures. At least they can use their good offices to invite, particularly the Isle of Man, which shares the Celtic, Viking heritage of the Republic of Ireland and whose language was rescued by Eamon De Valera in the early 1950s. I hope that everyone will reflect on the point.

This is not the first time that I have raised this point. I raised it with a Minister a long time ago—not this Minister. That Minister was a mediocre one, who pompously said, "It is a matter for the Irish Republic to apply." That made me very cross, and still does today. I know that we will get a different response, however. One of the things that all organisations do—it does not matter if they are the Boy Scouts, the Townswomen's Guilds, the Reform Club or a workingmen's club—is to extend invitations to people who they think can contribute and whose presence would be valuable. They do it as a way of extending to those people their respect for them. That is why I think that an invitation should be extended to the Irish Republic.

There might be a residual one or two people who do not think that such an invitation ought not to come from the United Kingdom. So be it. Let this Minister say that he will work with Canada, Australia, New Zealand, South Africa, the Caribbean countries and the countries around the world to see whether they should take the initiative of inviting the Irish Republic to take its natural place in the Commonwealth of nations.

An End To 60 Years of Separation?

By Jerry Walsh
Reform Member, London

The question "Ireland & the Commonwealth: an end to 60 years of separation?" was discussed at a meeting of the Royal Commonwealth Society at the Commonwealth Club, 25 Northumberland Avenue, London WC2N 5AP on Tuesday 25 November 2008 at 6.15pm. The meeting was introduced by Lord Rana. The Panel members were Dame Veronica Sutherland, Dr Ian Paisley and Mr Des O'Malley.

In his introduction, Lord Rana said he had pursued the question of Ireland joining the New Commonwealth which arose from the 1949 London Agreement, but Ireland had withdrawn only 8 days before. Various Secretaries General of the Commonwealth have visited Ireland, North & South.

The first to speak was former UK Ambassador in Dublin 1995-1999 and former Commonwealth Deputy Secretary General Dame Veronica Sutherland. She outlined her affection both for Ireland & the Commonwealth Secretariat. The Commonwealth consists of 53 countries, rich & poor, bound by history and language. Each country is equal. The organisation is no longer the British Commonwealth and London is no longer the centre. The Harare Declaration 1991 sets out the standards expected of Commonwealth members. A small Ministerial group deals with departures from these standards. The modern Commonwealth concerns itself with many issues including: debt relief; a Commonwealth funded permanent representation for smaller countries at the UN, health care, training judges, human rights and due democratic processes. In 1998 there was an exploratory meeting in Dublin. She admitted there are strong feelings on both sides of the "joining" argument in Ireland.

Describing himself as a Unionist of the strongest persuasion, Dr. Ian Paisley spoke next. He advocates Irish membership of the Commonwealth and many of the 53 members of the Commonwealth feel Ireland should be in. Ireland has nothing to give up by membership. The Commonwealth makes an important contribution to today's world.

Mr Des O'Malley spoke last. Noting that the Commonwealth was about to celebrate its 60th birthday, he said Ireland had never been a member of THIS Commonwealth and the gap between Ireland's membership of the previous Commonwealth and this one was only 8 days. He said that Ireland looks on the EU as its most important international involvement but there has been the recent hiccup of the Lisbon Treaty. He mentioned Ireland's membership of the UN, the OSCE and the Council of Europe. He suggested that few countries enjoy a closer relationship than the UK and Ireland and that Ireland enjoys a good relationship with all 53 states of the Commonwealth. He said he cannot summon up an impetus personally in favour of Ireland joining the Commonwealth. He feared that Irish membership of the Commonwealth might resurrect quiescent passions and that he prefers to leave baggage from a bygone era behind us. Des O'Malley concluded his contribution with a quote from the historian JJ Lee from UCC: "reflecting on the departure from the Commonwealth, it seems doubtful on the whole if Irish absence made much difference to Ireland or to the Commonwealth".

Following the conclusion of the contributions from the formal speakers, there were comments and questions from the floor.

Mark Robinson from the RCS would take issue with Des O'Malley over value added – Ireland has a tremendous amount to offer the Commonwealth in the new Commonwealth. Irish Ambassadors are usually to be found on the margins of Commonwealth meetings. There is no image in Ireland of the modern Commonwealth. Ireland plays a similar role in the world. More publicity is needed in Ireland about what the Commonwealth does.

Lord Rana said that he had been having a one-man crusade on this issue. He said that DesO'Malley covered the British-Irish relationship, but not the relationship between Ireland and the Commonwealth. India serves as a good example. Commonwealth membership would help relations between Ireland and India. There are huge advantages in trade and education. The Commonwealth will be changing rapidly. Ireland needs to look at the Commonwealth as a whole.

In reply, Des O'Malley said that there is no antipathy in Ireland, but there is no enthusiasm either. However, Irish people have a great capacity to manufacture antipathy.

The Mozambique High Commissioner described his country as the newest member of the Commonwealth. The Commonwealth played an important role in the peace process in Mozambique an also in development there. Mozambique has used the Commonwealth as a platform to acquire investment and technology. He urged those present to pause and imagine a world without the organisation.

Annie Winter described herself as an Irish citizen working in the Commonwealth Trade Union sector. She suggested that the big problem is the perception of the Commonwealth in Ireland. The close association with the Queen and the fact that the Commonwealth Office is in London are problems. But, these are problems for Australia and for other parts of the Commonwealth for the same reasons.

Various other comments from the floor included that one of the strengths of the modern Commonwealth is the multiplicity of diverse organisations within the Commonwealth and that Commonwealth bodies need to forge links with their counterparts in Ireland – bridge-building!

Concluding, Baroness Prashar, Chair of the Royal Commonwealth Society said that this had been a constructive informative debate. She felt the message from the meeting was to work around perceptions. She wondered how to get across to people what the Commonwealth stands for? She said the modern Commonwealth has a great deal to offer today's world and that we need to raise the profile of the Commonwealth in Ireland.

The Commonwealth at 60

By Gordon Lucy & John Erskine

The modern Commonwealth was 60 years old in 2009. Commonwealth Day (the second Monday in March every year) marked the 60th anniversary of the London Declaration, the birth certificate of the modern Commonwealth, in 1949. The theme for Commonwealth Day this year was 'The Commonwealth @ 60 – serving a new generation', an appropriate theme since young people under the age of 25 make up half of the two billion people who constitute the population of the Commonwealth. The modern Commonwealth consists of 54 member states, brought together by a shared commitment to international understanding and cooperation, the promotion of democracy, the alleviation of poverty, the sharing of expertise and the search for peace. These are among the objectives contained in 'The Declaration of Commonwealth Principles'. Member states, rich and poor, small and large, come from all round the world. The Commonwealth provides a forum particularly for smaller nations and a voice for their concerns. The Commonwealth is supported by a permanent secretariat and its current Secretary-General is the former Indian diplomat, Kamalesh Sharma.

The Commonwealth Games offer an opportunity for international sporting participation and representation that complements other, and often more exclusive, international sporting occasions.

Unique global grouping

The London Declaration was both imaginative and innovative in a number of respects. It affirmed that King George VI would be recognised as 'the symbol' of the

Commonwealth association. Thus, it became possible for India to be a republic and to remove King George VI as head of their state, but yet to recognise him as Head of the Commonwealth. The Declaration also repeatedly emphasised the freedom and equality of its members, not only in their relationship to the Head of the Commonwealth as a 'free association of independent nations', but also stressed their shared 'pursuit of peace, liberty and progress'. It was also at this juncture that the prefix 'British' was dropped from the title. When King George VI died in February 1952, the Queen assumed the role of Head of the Commonwealth.

The Queen's affection for the Commonwealth is well known. She has often spoken of the importance of partnership and has recognized the nature of the modern Commonwealth as 'a unique global grouping'.

Although, historically, the Commonwealth grew out of the British Empire, it has not been the 'British' Commonwealth since 1949; and one of the Commonwealth's newest member states – Mozambique – is a former Portuguese rather than a British colony.

Rwanda, the most recent member state to join, is a former Belgian colony.

A triumph over division

The Commonwealth is a truly remarkable organisation. Chief Anyaoku, who was Secretary-General of the Commonwealth between 1990 and 2000, has observed:

> The Commonwealth is a triumph of true human interests over the divisions of race, colour, culture and religion ... it represents a principle that transcends narrow interests and divisions and ... works to translate the concept of common humanity into a living reality.

Sixty years ago the Commonwealth, apart from the United Kingdom, consisted of seven self-governing nations: Canada, Australia, New Zealand, South Africa, India, Pakistan and Ceylon (now Sri Lanka).

During the last 60 years later, a greatly expanded Commonwealth has become a unique family of 54 member countries, accounting for almost two billion people – one third of the world's population. Sixteen countries have the Queen has their head of state, five countries have their own national monarchs and 33 are republics. Twenty-nine member countries are classified as 'small states' with a population of less than 1.5 million. Over 50% of Commonwealth citizens are under 25 years old. The Commonwealth includes some of the world's richest and poorest nations. A very high proportion of Commonwealth citizens live on less than 50p per day.

Geographically, the Commonwealth is strongly represented in west and southern Africa and Asia, embraces almost all of the Caribbean and much of the Pacific, as well as having members in the Mediterranean, Europe and North America.

In the United Kingdom, unfortunately, the importance and value of the Commonwealth are too often insufficiently recognised, as John Simpson, the World Affairs Editor of BBC News, has conceded:

> 'Nowadays, it is only the British who sneer at the Commonwealth ... for the smaller

developing states, the great majority of Commonwealth members, it is the best way of getting international attention for their concerns'.

Other Commonwealth countries appreciate and value the shared commitment to democracy, the alleviation of poverty and the search for peace.

Partnership and development
As the Queen is the first to recognise, the true value of the Commonwealth lies in its role as a global network which promotes partnership between both governments and peoples. Much of its strength comes from the work of voluntary groups and professional bodies and their exchange programmes and development initiatives. These activities give practical expression to the Commonwealth ideal of friendship and co-operation, and provide real benefits for ordinary people in areas as diverse as health care, economic development and the protection of the environment.

In the 1950s Lester Pearson, politician, diplomat, and Prime Minister of Canada, who was prominent as a mediator in international disputes in the 1960s, warned that humans were moving into 'an age when different civilizations will have to learn to live side by side in peaceful interchange, learning from each other, studying each other's history and ideals and art and culture, mutually enriching each other's lives. The alternative, in this overcrowded little world, is misunderstanding, tension, clash and catastrophe.'

Lester Pearson's prescient words are as relevant today as they were more than half a century ago and the Commonwealth, 60 years on, offers a unique experience as a role model for international relations.[8]

---

[8] This article was published in *News Letter,* March 2009.

The Queen's Commonwealth Day Message 2009

This year the Commonwealth commemorates its foundation sixty years ago. The London Declaration of 1949 was the start of a new era in which our member countries committed themselves to work together, in partnership and as equals, towards a shared future.

We can rightly celebrate the fact that the founding members' vision of the future has become a reality. The Commonwealth has evolved out of all recognition from its beginning. It has helped give birth to modern nations, and the eight original countries have become fifty-three. We are now home to nearly two billion people, a third of the world's population. Across continents and oceans, we have come to represent all the rich diversity of humankind.

Yet despite its size and scale, the Commonwealth to me has been sustained during all this change by the continuity of our mutual values and goals. Our beliefs in freedom, democracy and human rights; development and prosperity mean as much today as they did more than half a century ago.

These values come from a common responsibility exercised by our governments and peoples. It is this which makes the Commonwealth a family of nations and peoples, at ease with being together. As a result, I believe we are inspired to do our best to meet people's most pressing needs, and to develop a truly global perspective. That is why the modern Commonwealth has stood the test of time.

But as we reflect upon our long association, we should recognize the challenges that lie ahead. Nearly one billion people of today's Commonwealth are under 25 years of age.

These are the people that this association must continue to serve in the future. It is they who can help shape the Commonwealth of today, and whose children will inherit the Commonwealth of tomorrow.

To help them make the best of their opportunities, our young men and women therefore need the opportunity to become active and responsible members of the communities in which they live. I am pleased that the Commonwealth recognizes this, and is determined to continue to put young people at its centre.

The call that brought the Commonwealth together in 1949 remains the same today. Then we joined together in a collective spirit – built on lasting principles, wisdom, energy and creativity – to meet the great tasks of our times. As the Commonwealth celebrates its sixtieth birthday, its governments, communities and we as individuals should welcome that achievement. Together, we should continue to work hard to deal with today's challenges so that the young people of today's Commonwealth can realize their aspirations. In that way, we can look to the future with confidence.

Celebrating the Commonwealth at 60

By Kamalesh Sharma

Commonwealth Secretary-General

The 26 April 2009 marked the 60th anniversary of the London Declaration , when the modern Commonwealth was born. What was the Declaration? What is its significance and why are we celebrating?

Before the Declaration

The origins of the Commonwealth stretch back much further than 60 years but 1949 marks the pivotal point at which the Commonwealth's colonial legacy was positively transformed into a partnership based on equality, choice and consensus. Prior to this the Balfour Declaration of 1926 had established all member countries as 'equal in status to one another, in no way subordinate one to another', and this was in turn adopted into law with the 1931 Statute of Westminster. However it was India's desire to adopt a republican form of constitution while simultaneously retaining its link with the Commonwealth that prompted a radical reconsideration of the terms of association.

No longer the British Commonwealth

In April 1949, Heads of Government from Australia, Britain, Ceylon, India, New Zealand, Pakistan, South Africa and the Canadian Secretary of State for External Affairs met in London and deliberated over six days. The outcome was the Declaration of London.

Their final communiqué was both innovative and bold in a number of ways. It stated that King George VI would be recognised as 'the symbol' the Commonwealth association. Thus India could remove King George VI as head of their state but recognise him as Head of the Commonwealth. The Declaration also repeatedly emphasised the freedom and equality of its members not just in their relationship to the Head of the Commonwealth as a 'free association of [..] independent nations' but also in their cooperative 'pursuit of peace, liberty and progress'. It was also at this juncture that the prefix British was dropped from the title. When King George VI died, Queen Elizabeth II assumed the role of Head of the Commonwealth.

After the end of World War II the Commonwealth became the natural association of choice for many of the new nations emerging out of decolonisation. Starting with Ghana in 1957, the Commonwealth expanded rapidly with new members from Africa, the Caribbean, the Mediterranean and the Pacific.

Why are we celebrating?

The Commonwealth is now a unique association of 53 independent states consulting and co-operating in the common interests of their peoples and in the promotion of international understanding. It comprises countries from all major continents of the world, rich and poor, small and large. In the 60 years since the Declaration, the relevance and value of the relationship has repeatedly been reaffirmed and consolidated.

The creation of the Commonwealth Secretariat in 1965 and the ever expanding number of professional and advocacy Commonwealth organisations reflect this; but most significant is the expansion of membership from 8 in 1949 to 53 in 2009. A clear demonstration of how the scope of the Declaration ensured that the Commonwealth retained a relevance to other newly independent nations.

In many ways the 'atmosphere of goodwill and mutual understanding' in which the Declaration was formulated can be seen as the crucible in which the character governing the Commonwealth today was created. It balanced modern realities with the pragmatic and the positive, which is why 30% of the world's population have cause for celebration in 2009. Nearly two billion people now live in the Commonwealth, and half of these are under 25. The future of the Commonwealth belongs with young people, and this is why the Commonwealth theme for 2009 is 'thecommonwealth@60 - serving a new generation'.

IRELAND:

TIME TO COME HOME

BY SIR SHRIDATH RAMPHAL
FORMER COMMONWEALTH SECRETARY-GENERAL (1975-1990)

Speech given at the Round Table Dinner on the occasion of the 2009 Commonwealth Summit in Port of Spain, Trinidad.

If you find this speech interesting, you may also like to visit the comprehensive website of the Ramphal Centre for Commonwealth Studies - which helps to promote the essential values of the Commonwealth; good governance, economic development and social justice around the world. Mr Chairman, Members of the Round Table, Commonwealth kin –

May I be permitted to begin – despite our sequestration on the Campus of the University – by extending in absentia to Her Majesty and Prince Philip the warmest of welcomes to the Caribbean, and invite you to join me in a toast to the Head of the Commonwealth and her Consort: The Queen!

Next, let me say in a preliminary way that when invited to speak after dinner I was not circumscribed in any way by theme or issue – a luxury I do not often enjoy. I intend, therefore to speak to a matter that has long been on my mind and which I may not have again as good an opportunity to raise. It is eminently relevant to the 60th anniversary of the birth of the modern Commonwealth in 1949 and, I invite you to agree, to the Commonwealth's years beyond 60. To that end, I have called these remarks which I assure you will not detain you beyond legitimate post-prandial allowance: 'Ireland: Time to Come Home'. But, before that, there are some linked observations.

When Richard Bourne first approached me about this evening's Dinner I was frankly hesitant: an instinct about old wine and new wineskins made me pause. But reflection trumped instinct. The Round Table after all is an even older bottle than my wine; and it is the Round Table with whom I am here to dine. In any case, if I might stay with my metaphoric wine, the Commonwealth is like vintage port, its intrinsic quality doesn't alter with changing decanters. So here I am, on the margins of the Commonwealth Heads of Government Meeting – if it still is that - in my native Caribbean, thanking you for asking me. And I do sincerely thank you; for if the Commonwealth is a 'Club' –as African member states insistently describe it - the Round Table comes close to being an unofficial patron, and like any good patron, never far from the Commonwealth's fortunes.

The eve of your Centennial is a proud time and I am happy to share it with you. 1910 was worlds away. That you can rightly boast of being Britain's oldest international affairs Journal tells not only a story of your vintage, but also of the eras that have come and gone since the Round table first convened. And in all that changing time you have kept faith and focus with the Commonwealth idea in all of its evolving modes; helping, indeed, to shape them through the rigour of intellectual analysis and commentary.

To have done that for a hundred years is a huge accomplishment; and I am sure that through all your time of celebration you will be recalling the stalwarts that founded and presided in myriad ways over the affairs of the Round Table – and of your trusteeship of their legacy. In my time in Marlborough House I was ever grateful for the Round Table's contribution to the Commonwealth project. It is a dimension of Commonwealth affairs whose absence we would bemoan were it not there. I wish, of course, that the Journal is more widely disseminated – particularly in the rest of the Commonwealth; but since this is a wish I assume you share, I expect its fulfillment is a work in progress.

This year, the Commonwealth has been celebrating its own Jubilee within those hundred years – 60 years of the modern Commonwealth – 60 years of a Commonwealth experience made possible by the wisdom that prevailed among Commonwealth leaders in 1949 – as the Round Table itself neared 40. The Head of the Commonwealth, Her Majesty the Queen, held a celebratory Reception this year to mark the occasion, and we had the pleasure of looking at the original photographs of the 1949 Prime Ministers grouped around King George VI. The Secretary-General (along with Emeka Anyaoku and me) were photographed with Her Majesty at the same spot in the Palace where that earlier photograph had been taken with her father 60 years earlier. I took the opportunity of assuring Her Majesty, of the awareness of many of the quiet role the King had played in 1949 in facilitating that enlightened decision of leaders of the quality of Clement Atlee, Jawaharalal Nehru, Lester Pearson (not yet Prime Minister) and their colleagues.

I have spoken elsewhere of that April Declaration and its making of the modern Commonwealth; members of the Round Table need no reminder of that moment of great vision, but as we dine tonight we should lift a glass to that moment when the Commonwealth faced with a turning in the road took the 'path less travelled by' and by doing so made all the difference to the future of the Commonwealth, and in a small way, to the future of the world. Such moments do not come often in the affairs of nations, and more rarely still, such an impeccably right choice. It is a time to remember the enlightenment of the great men who made it – both in Downing Street and in the Palace. And in remembering, let us be encouraged to look out for other turnings in the road, and other roads less travelled by, which taken might lead to lush pastures for the Commonwealth.

The April Declaration in this sense was a moment of pleasure; but, Shelley was right, sometimes 'our sincerest laughter with some little pain is fraught'. And it is on this that I would like to dwell a little; for the pain lingers and can, and I believe should, be relieved. I talk of Ireland – not, I know, on the Agenda of the Port of Spain Meeting, and not in our minds 60 years after it left the Commonwealth; for this year marks the Jubilee of that event too.

Four days before the London Summit opened in April 1949 Ireland had left Commonwealth, baulking at 'allegiance' to the Crown and assuming Commonwealth membership to be incompatible with Republican Status. That the Republic of Ireland Act was passed in December 1948 but only brought into force four days before the London Summit opened, suggests however that that assumption may not have been unquestioned in Dublin. In other words, for the new Irish Republic, leaving the Commonwealth was not so much a legal necessity (a necessary implication of becoming a Republic) but a deliberate political choice. And, of course, my point tonight, is that political choices are never for all time.

I must say a little more, however; and some of it really is ironic. Historically, the Irish Free State helped to make the modern Commonwealth possible through its contributions to the Imperial Conferences of 1926 and 1930 which gave the Commonwealth legal definition. The insistent and constructive efforts of the Cosgrave Government were central to both the Balfour Declaration of 1926 and the Statute of Westminster of 1931. In 1926 both South Africa and the Irish Free State claimed credit for securing the definition of 'Dominion Status'. To the statement of General Hertzog on his return to South Africa: 'We have brought home the bacon'; the Irish Representative Kevin O'Higgins is reported to have commented: 'Irish bacon'. And so too was the Statute of Westminster. Nicholas Mansergh was actually shown the desk in Dublin where the Statute was said to have been drafted. The point is, Ireland played a major role in moving the Commonwealth to modernity. But the sticking point still was 'allegiance'

Not surprisingly, when in 1948 India decided to become a Republic but wished to remain in the Commonwealth, it was to Dublin's long efforts to work out appropriate forms that it turned; and this time the whole Commonwealth and its future direction benefited. In a sense, all India did was to declare her intention to become a Republic, express her wish to remain in the Commonwealth and her acceptance of the King as the symbol of the free association of the Commonwealth's independent member states and, as such, Head of the Commonwealth.

But a sea change had occurred. The effect of the April Declaration was to replace allegiance to the Crown as the criterion of Commonwealth membership with the much more modest acceptance of the King, later the Queen, as Head of the Commonwealth. Today, Commonwealth Heads of Government meet in a Republic in the Caribbean. This apparently simple change removed at one stroke the legal objection that had caused the Irish Republic's withdrawal a week earlier; but whether it would have made Ireland's continued membership likely had it come earlier is another matter entirely.

Sean MacBride's view – and he was Ireland's Foreign Minister at time (Minister for External Affairs in the Inter-Party Government - when I asked him the question many years later, was decidedly negative. He explained that, In fact, the date for bringing the Republic of Ireland Act into force had been long set for Easter Day 1949, viz., 18 April; the convening of the London Summit on 22 April simply galvanized Dublin into not letting the date slip. Republicans, like MacBride wanted no reason to arise that might encourage second thoughts. The truth was, that the long and troubled relationship between Dublin and London and the powerful symbolism of the Crown, despite the disappearance of 'allegiance', was not enough <u>at that time</u> to stay the process of withdrawal from the Commonwealth. Yet, 60 years later, Dublin's fear that Commonwealth membership might tarnish its independence has not been the experience of other Commonwealth countries, the great majority of them republics. Rather the opposite. Nehru, himself arch-nationalist and republican, described Commonwealth membership as 'independence plus'.

Six decades later, when some of the wounds of the troubles are healing under the influence of Dublin and London working together; when the Queen as the symbolic Head of the Commonwealth has demonstrated beyond question that the Commonwealth's Republics are as one with any other; when the Commonwealth is opening up its membership to newcomers who share none of the historic ties that bind Ireland to so many of us; is it perhaps time to tell Ireland that nothing but welcome awaits her in the Commonwealth when she feels ready to come home.

I thought that the Caribbean might not be so bad a place to raise this matter in that there is a kinship with Ireland whose roots go deep in history – deep in the conjunctures between the experience of Ireland and that of many of the countries of the Commonwealth. The 'provinces' in the beginning were not so very different from the colonies of settlement. When I read, for example, that Lord Montgomery's family background was in 'the Plantation' – a plantation as much human as agricultural – we are on common ground. My forbears from India were indentured to the plantations of British Guiana, where 'plantation' meant colonization, as well a human transplantation to a form of servitude.

So let me end with a conjuncture of a lighter kind. When, in 1837, the Guiana sugar planters were pressing for British government acquiescence in bringing indentured workers from India, they used as part of their argument the allegation that labourers imported from elsewhere, including 'Ireland', had not proved suitable " from the influence of the climate generally producing reluctance to labour, and increasing the Desire for Spirituous Liquors, which the low Price and abundance of new Rum enables them to gratify". I quote from a letter from Sir John Gladstone, the father of England's future Prime Minister.

My ancestors went to Guyana's sugar plantations as a result of that letter – whence by indirection I come to you tonight. Lest the Irish in Guyana be defamed, let me add that it was not so much the indentured labourers – from Ireland or elsewhere – who gratified a desire for 'Spirituours Liquors', but the sugar planters themselves who made famous that most potent of tonics – the 'Demerara rum swizzle' – the progenitor of the 'West Indian Rum Punch', which I hope you have enjoyed copiously in Port of Spain.

It is time these Commonwealth conjunctures with Ireland and the Irish fulfilled their innate destiny.

Where better to say this that to the Round Table - and in the Caribbean!

Time to Return

By Roy Garland
PEACE ACTIVIST AND IRISH NEWS COLUMNIST

The time has surely come for the Irish Republic to seriously consider returning to the Commonwealth. This would add to the message that old animosities are being forgotten and the Republic is becoming a place where different traditions and identities meet and mingle in peace, safety and equality.

Moves towards reconciliation have faced stern resistance from, among others, Ian Paisley who paradoxically became first minister in cahoots with Bertie Ahern and Martin McGuinness. The very word reconciliation was rejected as a ploy of the enemy comparable to the proverbial spider welcoming the hapless fly into its cosy parlour. Reconciliation was depicted as a one way street towards domination by Rome and subservience to a nationalist agenda.

But reconciliation cannot mean the end of differences. That would be absorption whereas reconciliation entails acceptance of differences making them less divisive. Those nationalists who violently reject anything other than a 32 county mono-cultural Irish state hostile to Britain plainly do not seek reconciliation. But re-entering the Commonwealth does not mean a return to subservience but new relationships as envisaged in the Anglo-Irish Agreement, Good Friday Agreement, St Andrews' and the British Irish Council. It could encourage a new version of an ancient vision by which Irish people contribute to a better world.

Republicans feared British imperialism but many unionists feared a kind of religious Catholic imperialism. Catholic doctrines were enshrined in the Irish Constitution. The sale of contraceptives was declared illegal while divorce was unconstitutional. Claims on the territory of the six counties were experienced as threatening and imperialistic. While most imperialism has positive and negative aspects we tend to emphasise the positive in our own and the negative in other people's imperialism. Protestants believed the Catholic Church kept their people in ignorance while Irish nationalists believed the British kept the Irish people in slavery.

Despite changes, some unionists still regard the Republic as a threatening alien state. Some have never crossed into the south just as some southerners have never seen the black north. When I asked a unionist politician to address a private meeting in Dundalk he agreed but then reneged, saying he feared being shot by the IRA.

A minority of northern Protestants always visited the Republic but others, including my dad, refused point blank. He and mum visited the old Monaghan homestead in the 1920s by pony and trap but never returned. I grew up with horror stories about life on the other side and faced a difficult journey to overcome that bitter legacy. Louth historian Harold O'Sullivan was prominent among those who introduced me to the world of my ancestors that is long gone. They survived as Anglo-Irish Catholics through centuries of turmoil until the religious wars of the 17th century after which they survived as staunch Orange Protestants in Monaghan.

County Louth is peppered with the lingering remnants of old English families whose story was particularly tragic. Despite their contribution to modern Ireland, some became more Irish than the Irish while others retained pride in their English/Norman heritage even if it was kept under wraps. My warring ancestors lived and died in no-man's land between Irish and English Uriel (Monaghan and Louth) occasionally forming alliances but also fighting with their neighbours.

Today I see the Irish Republic in a different light even though aspects of that state, including the preamble to the constitution, overtly exclude people like me whose ancestors might have been Irish patriots but probably never Irish nationalists. Yet I no longer feel alienated from the "grey skies of an Irish Republic" and can feel at home in either jurisdiction. Further dialogue, experience and actions are necessary to remove the remaining barriers. If the south was to re-enter the Commonwealth, the log jam might be broken, hurts might heal more quickly and new relationships grow more strongly.

The modern international, multi-cultural Commonwealth consisting of 54 independent states, many of which are republics, exists to serve common interests and promote international understanding and peace. It represents thirty per cent of the world's population and includes a very broad range of faiths, cultures and traditions. Irish people have many ties with the Commonwealth and re-joining would give expression to relationships that already exist. It might free unionists from the shackles of siege mentality that almost denies their Irish heritage. But their deep attachment to Britain and the Ulster Scots heritage need not and cannot be bartered to enable them to appreciate their Irish inheritance as well.

IRELAND AND THE COMMONWEALTH

MEMBER STATES

54 Independent states working together in the common interests of their citizens for development, democracy and peace.

Antigua and Barbuda	Jamaica	St Lucia	
Australia	Kenya	St Vincent and the Grenadines	
The Bahamas	Kiribati	Samoa	
Bangladesh	Lesotho	Seychelles	
Barbados	Malawi	Sierra Leone	
Belize	Malaysia	Singapore	
Botswana	Maldives	Solomon Islands	
Brunei Darussalam	Malta	South Africa	
Cameroon	Mauritius	Sri Lanka	
Canada	Mozambique	Swaziland	
Cyprus	Namibia	Tonga	
Dominica	Nauru**	Trinidad and Tobago	
Fiji Islands*	New Zealand	Tuvalu	
The Gambia	Nigeria	Uganda	
Ghana	Pakistan	United Kingdom	
Grenada	Papua New Guinea	United Republic of Tanzania	
Guyana	Rwanda	Vanuatu	
India	St Kitts and Nevis	Zambia	

*Following the decisions taken by the Commonwealth Ministerial Action Group on 31 July 2009, Fiji Islands was suspended from membership of the Commonwealth on 1 September 2009 **Nauru is a Member in Arrears

IRELAND AND THE COMMONWEALTH

The Commonwealth and its members